The Dyslexia Workbook for Adults

THE
DYSLEXIA
WORKBOOK
FOR ADULTS

Practical Tools to Improve Executive Functioning,
Boost Literacy Skills, and Develop Your Unique Strengths

GAVIN REID, PhD

ROCKRIDGE PRESS

I would like to dedicate this book to all adults with dyslexia—for their courage, tenacity, and talents. By displaying their strengths, they have helped to establish an attitude shift in education and employment, which has greatly benefited society at large. It has been a privilege for me to be a part of this movement and I have been enriched personally and professionally through meeting and working with countless children and adults with dyslexia.

For general information on our other products and services or to obtain technical support, please contact our Customer Care Department within the United States at (866) 744-2665, or outside the United States at (510) 253-0500.

Rockridge Press publishes its books in a variety of electronic and print formats. Some content that appears in print may not be available in electronic books, and vice versa.

Interior and Cover Designer: Darren Samuel
Art Producer: Karen Williams and Sue "Bees" Bischofberger
Editor: Lori Tenny

All images used under license from Shutterstock.com; bird photographs on pp. 73 and 74 courtesy of Rodger Shearer. Author photo courtesy of Peter Dibdin

ISBN: Print 978-1-64739-867-5 | eBook 978-1-64739-545-2
R0

Contents

Introduction

Welcome to this workbook about dyslexia in adults. I am delighted to have the opportunity to write this book and hope that it speaks to many of the questions you have, whether you've been diagnosed with dyslexia or suspect you could be living with it. For 30 years now, I've been a psychologist, and before that I was a classroom teacher. I've specialized in dyslexia for most of that time. I'll provide clear pointers to help you progress in many areas so you can realize your full strengths and true potential.

When I was at school, dyslexia wasn't something that was diagnosed, and I'm certain very few, if any, of the teachers had even heard the term. I suppose I was self-diagnosed, but I did not come to that realization until much later. I can recall totally switching off when the teacher switched on. I needed to see and discuss, not listen. Though I didn't realize it at the time, I was an active learner in a passive learning environment.

I am fortunate that I have a good long-term memory. But the flip side of this is that my short-term memory can be quite woeful! This did not go unnoticed by my mother, who was always astounded on the very few occasions I came home from the local grocery store with all of the correct items.

As I ventured into work, university, and teaching, I gradually realized I had a dyslexic profile and tried to compensate for it. But I still remember some glaring and embarrassing examples of my dyslexia in action. For example, after studying medieval history for three years, I still habitually misspelled the word *feudal* in my final exam papers, even though I'd probably used the word about 100 times during my course.

Dyslexia is an ongoing life experience—one that asks you to continue to adapt and grow. The important point is that dyslexia doesn't need to be a disadvantage, and in this book, I'll show you how dyslexia can be just the opposite—a genuine advantage. To help you make the most of that, this book offers opportunities for you to develop the know-how and the skills to cultivate your strengths and achieve success, however you define it.

Looking back, I can say that healthy self-esteem is perhaps one of the most crucial elements in the journey to personal fulfillment for people with dyslexia. This book will help you develop self-esteem, self-advocacy, and self-knowledge. It will also help you gain a sense of empowerment and a greater appreciation for the positive aspects of dyslexia.

I want to empower you to learn and develop your talents in a positive way and see your dyslexia as a pathway to develop new skills and enhance your existing strengths. The book will give you insights into your ways of thinking and learning. It will invite you to engage in stimulating activities to build the skills you want to improve and appreciate the skills you have that you may not have been aware of. View your dyslexia as a gift and use it like you would use all gifts—with care, compassion, and gratitude.

Let me assure you that legislation and equality laws are on your side. Federal law in the United States (and in most countries) formally recognizes dyslexia, and most states have dyslexia-specific laws. Research by nessy.com in 2019 and DyslexicAdvantage.org in 2020 indicated that only four states had no specific dyslexia laws. Although most of the legislation relates to schools and higher education, there is clearly a relation to adults in the workplace. Most of the legislation appears to focus on definitions of dyslexia, screening procedures, interventions, and accommodations. One of the benefits is that individuals with dyslexia will begin to see accommodations and general support for dyslexia as the norm and not something that is special or segregates them in any major way from others. Increasingly, the stigma of disability that may have been associated with dyslexia many years ago has become less of a factor. The work of the International Dyslexia Association (IDA) has been instrumental in gaining support for adults with dyslexia, and its annual conference has a powerful adult focus.

Although the Americans with Disabilities Act attempts to protect against discrimination in the workplace, the criteria are less clear than for schools. Essentially, employers have only to provide reasonable accommodations. It is worthwhile for adults to also seek advice from the Job Accommodation Network, which is a key source of free, expert, and confidential guidance on workplace accommodations and disability employment issues.

Despite this progress, powerful lobby groups, such as the IDA, still have a key role to play in this area. Nevertheless, you'll learn in this book that dyslexia can be seen as a differentiator that can be an advantage to the individual in many situations.

During my many years as a professional in the field of dyslexia, I have seen changes, and I have seen success. I'm happy to say the playing field is now more level than it previously was.

It's important to understand that dyslexia exists on a continuum from mild to severe. My view is that it doesn't really matter where you are on that continuum. What's important is how your dyslexia impacts you, your life, and your work. You may well be on the mild side of the continuum, but your dyslexia can still have a major impact on your work.

This workbook is for all adults with dyslexia. You will find a vast amount of activities to help you overcome the challenges of dyslexia, and the strength-building activities in this book will help you see your dyslexia as a gift, a strength, and a very important part of you. Treasure that!

How to Use This Workbook

As the title suggests, this is a workbook. You'll find a range of practical exercises and strategies with a twofold purpose: to help you recognize and work through the barriers and obstacles of dyslexia and to help you discover the strengths unique to dyslexic patterns of thinking and how to build upon them.

This workbook is for both individuals who want to go through the activities at their own pace and for collective use, such as in a support group for dyslexic adults. It's also for educators to use as supplementary material for their courses.

We'll start with information and explanations about dyslexia—what it is, the causes, the challenges, the strengths, and how people have used those strengths to succeed.

The following chapters provide practical activities that focus on improving your literacy skills. The benefits of these activities are supported by the most up-to-date, evidence-based research.

The book is comprehensive and acknowledges that adults with dyslexia can experience obstacles in addition to literacy issues. There is a chapter focusing on auditory, visual, and spatial exercises, as well as a chapter providing strategies to improve executive functioning, which can be described as the engine of the brain. Executive functioning is related to many of the challenges those with dyslexia experience.

Meanwhile, you'll find chapters devoted to exercises to build resilience and cope with stress, strategies to build upon the strengths of dyslexia, and real-life scenarios of people with dyslexia who have overcome obstacles and utilized their strengths in their professional and personal lives. It is my hope that whatever profession you are in, regardless of your age, you will benefit from these and personally connect with this information and the associated scenarios.

Feel free to jump to any portion of the book that's appropriate to your situation. It's not necessary to go through the chapters in order. I encourage you to review the activities after you've completed them and make note of how you have progressed.

CHAPTER ONE

DYSLEXIA AND YOU

Dyslexia is one of the most well-known, but perhaps most misunderstood, conditions, mainly because dyslexia includes many characteristics beyond literacy issues.

Many adults with dyslexia can find themselves frustrated and confused because of the challenges they may face. They may compare themselves unfavorably with others, which of course is not a healthy situation. This book will help adults with dyslexia appreciate their strengths, encourage their creativity, and look at dyslexia in a positive way. I will be focusing as much on what you can do as on what you find difficult.

This chapter will provide an overview of dyslexia, dispel some of the misconceptions and myths about dyslexia, and explore the ways dyslexia may be impacting you as an adult. I'll discuss not only the challenges you may be experiencing in the workplace and elsewhere, but also the strengths of dyslexia and how you can use them to your advantage. I want to emphasize that dyslexia can be an ability and not a disability. Understanding your own dyslexic profile can be one of the keys to success.

To that end, this chapter will explain how dyslexia is diagnosed and provide pointers for self-assessment.

Dyslexia in Adults

The challenges and obstacles people with dyslexia face can be universal and lifelong. But it's important to recognize that they need not be defeating! Beyond the hurdles you may have ahead, it's important to realize the remarkable strengths inherent in dyslexic patterns of thinking and learn how to best use those to your advantage throughout adulthood. Throughout this book, we'll focus on enabling adults with dyslexia and promoting an ethos of positive self-esteem that paves the way for acceptance and success.

As an adult with dyslexia, you are unique. You face some of the same challenges experienced by younger people with dyslexia, yet you have a completely different set of obstacles in addition to different ways to use your remarkable strengths to your advantage throughout adulthood. Many areas of strength can be associated with dyslexia, such as thinking outside the box, problem-solving, visual perception, creativity, and social skills, not to mention self-reliance and determination.

I am sure you experienced many hurdles at some points during your school years. You may have received support or developed your own strategies, but you also may have felt overwhelmed by the obstacles you faced. Whatever age you are and whatever career stage you are in, take heart! You have the ability to overcome the challenges of dyslexia, and I sincerely hope this workbook gives you the means to do so.

Although there are numerous materials, programs, books, and videos that are aimed at helping adults with dyslexia, not all dyslexic adults are the same or share the same challenges. I see dyslexia as an *individual* set of characteristics. The degree and extent of these characteristics are unique to you. For that reason, you'll find it most helpful to respond to the tasks and approach the information in this workbook in your own way and at your own pace. This is important because every person with dyslexia is different, and you know yourself best.

Dyslexia Defined

There are many definitions of dyslexia, but most are very similar and have some core elements. It is also important to appreciate that dyslexia is a continuum of learning differences, with characteristics ranging from mild to severe. This means that not all adults with dyslexia will show exactly the same characteristics or have the same degree of difficulties. Dyslexia is almost like a constellation of features with some more prominent than others and more significant at certain times or with certain types of tasks. The most popular definition was developed by the International Dyslexia Association (IDA):

Dyslexia is a specific learning disability that is neurobiological in origin. It is characterized by difficulties with accurate and/or fluent word recognition and by poor spelling and decoding abilities. These difficulties typically result from a deficit in the phonological component of language that is often unexpected in relation to other cognitive abilities and the provision of effective classroom instruction. Secondary consequences may include problems in reading comprehension and reduced reading experience that can impede growth of vocabulary and background knowledge.

The key aspect of this definition is that people are born dyslexic! Dyslexia is driven by biological, not environmental, factors that affect how the brain is used. It is also worth noting that although dyslexia affects reading accuracy, there are other factors such as reading fluency, comprehension, retrieving background information, and vocabulary acquisition that are also impacted.

Additionally, some other definitions also emphasize processing difficulties, and reading is a subset of these. Although processing difficulties are a manifestation of dyslexia, they are not necessarily specific to dyslexia, and some people may well have processing difficulties due to other factors and syndromes and not necessarily be dyslexic. Examples of processing difficulties include the following:

- Poor short-term and working memory

- Difficulty remembering lists of information, even short lists or short instructions

- Poor long-term memory/organizational difficulties

- Difficulty planning written work

- Difficulty recalling a sequence of events and relating it in oral or written form

Causes of Dyslexia

Let's be very clear that dyslexia is not related to brain damage or low intelligence. While dyslexia is a biological disorder, cognitive, behavioral, and environmental factors play a significant role in the degree to which dyslexia impacts the individual.

Dyslexia is a neurobiological condition that can result from an interplay of genetics; atypical brain development; and perceptual, linguistic, and cognitive factors. Studies of the brain suggest that the brains of people with dyslexia are wired differently. Imagine your brain is like a computer. There are differences among computers: Some have fast processors. Some have huge memories. Others have slower processors, or their memory fills quickly and they operate at a different speed. But the important point is that they all work. And they can do what you want them to do!

The advances in MRI and other forms of brain imagery have been of great benefit to the scientific understanding of dyslexia, and understanding the science will help you understand an individual with dyslexia. Dyslexia is an inherited learning difference. Studies suggest there are at least nine genes that make someone vulnerable to problems with reading. These genes influence how the brain processes language and maps visual symbols into spoken words.

Learning is a lifelong process, and all brains are ready to learn. The dyslexic brain is especially ready to accept this challenge!

DYSLEXIA: MYTH VERSUS FACT

I mentioned earlier that dyslexia is perhaps the most well known of the constellation of learning issues, but the least understood. This is because there are many myths about dyslexia. Some of these have been around for such a long time that people with little knowledge of dyslexia start to believe them. I always started seminars by asking the audience what their perception of dyslexia is, and I was always amazed at the wide range of responses. Some of these are shown here alongside the truth.

MYTH	FACT
It's okay. You will grow out of dyslexia!	Dyslexia can be managed, certainly, but it is always there. Management of dyslexia is key. If it is successfully managed, its impact will be minimized and may not even be apparent.
Dyslexia does not exist—it is a social construct!	There is a significant body of research on dyslexia that offers very robust findings about the nature of dyslexia, and there are a number of peer-reviewed academic journals on dyslexia that are well respected by the scientific community. If you still have any doubts, ask any adult with dyslexia, teacher of children, or parent of a dyslexic child.
People with dyslexia cannot read.	This is not the case. The majority of adults with dyslexia can read, although some may continue to have reading challenges. Often in adulthood reading fluency is the main issue, which means it takes longer to read and process the print. This can have implications for reading comprehension. It's also important to note that dyslexia is not just a reading difficulty.

Diagnosing Dyslexia

Dyslexia is diagnosed by an experienced and registered psychologist. The psychologist obtains information from a number of sources, including background information on the client, and from a variety of tests.

It is not uncommon for dyslexia to overlap with other syndromes such as dysgraphia (handwriting difficulties), dyspraxia (coordination and movement difficulties), dyscalculia (math and number difficulties), and attention deficit hyperactivity disorder (ADHD or ADD). Comprehensive tests, together with background information, would inform the psychologist if the client's scoring pattern is representative of any of those syndromes.

A DYSLEXIA SELF-ASSESSMENT

Following is a questionnaire. Your answers can tell you if you're vulnerable to dyslexia, which means having many of the characteristics of dyslexia. This can explain why you're experiencing challenges in some areas. However, this self-assessment does not represent a formal diagnosis. It would be a good idea to obtain a more detailed assessment to confirm any diagnosis.

There are eight obstacle areas. If you answer "Yes" in more than four of them, you are likely vulnerable to dyslexia. You can give the Reading obstacle a higher weighting, and this can count as two.

(Please note: This is not a comprehensive test to self-diagnose dyslexia, and readers should consider an assessment by a professional if they haven't already been diagnosed.)

TYPE OF OBSTACLE	QUESTIONS	YES/NO
Memory	Do you have difficulty remembering auditory instructions and lists?	
	Do you have difficulty taking notes?	
Organization	Do you have difficulty remembering appointments, materials, and equipment you need to bring to work or meetings?	
Movement/ coordination	Did you or do you have difficulty with fine motor skills, such as tying shoelaces and handwriting?	
Reading	Do you have difficulty reading accurately or with reading speed or reading comprehension? Do you have difficulty pronouncing some words?	

(continued)

TYPE OF OBSTACLE	QUESTIONS	YES/NO
Spelling	Do you have difficulty remembering spelling rules and with spelling in general?	
Writing	Do you have difficulty starting a piece of written work, forming sentences, or developing an overall structure and organization for written work?	
Processing speed	Do you need more time to process information, such as receiving instructions from your manager, reading reports, and carrying out tasks in general?	
Numeracy	Do you have difficulty learning and/or remembering number facts or multiplication tables?	

The Challenges of Dyslexia

There is little doubt that early detection of dyslexia is beneficial in terms of putting the most appropriate teaching programs in place. If this takes place in the early years of education, it can prevent many of the learning hurdles that children with dyslexia experience during their school years. It can pave the way for classroom and exam accommodations and help to identify and maximize the student's strengths.

Perhaps most important, early detection can also prevent or at least minimize the feelings of failure and the resulting issues that stem from low self-esteem and a lack of confidence. When dyslexia is not diagnosed early, emotional challenges and frustration often result.

I've met many young adults in college and in the workplace who were never diagnosed. Baseball icon Nolan Ryan describes his school experience as frustrating and embarrassing. He was very shy in the classroom, and he found spelling extremely challenging. Many dyslexic adults relate on some level to what Ryan describes from his childhood.

One of the problems is that we often assess children's development by what they do, not by what they feel. The good news is that dyslexia is increasingly diagnosed early and addressing a child's learning challenges can begin when they're young.

In adulthood, dyslexia can lead to difficulty navigating professional and personal lives and reduced self-confidence. Adults with dyslexia tend to experience challenges in the following areas:

- **Reading.** One of the early challenges for children with dyslexia is mastering the sounds and symbols of language. This makes reading difficult for young children, and the early learning habits they acquire can stay with them as adults. Because they have difficulty in decoding print, they often learn to read by using context or guessing—sometimes remarkably accurately! This can be a useful strategy, but it can lend itself to misreading and misunderstanding the text. That's why adults with dyslexia have to reread, sometimes multiple times, to gain full and accurate comprehension. This requires sufficient time, which makes reading a major obstacle for some adults, particularly in certain work environments and at college.

- **Writing.** In the literacy arena, writing can present perhaps the biggest challenge. When speaking, adults with dyslexia can usually perform quite impressively, but when asked to write, they often have difficulties getting started. The difficulties lie in the area of structuring and organization, as well as with identifying the key points.

- **Verbal communication.** As mentioned, adults with dyslexia can be quite impressive when it comes to spoken communication, but they may well need some support with organizing a speech or relating the key points. Conversation and communication can become circular rather than direct. For some professions, such as filmmaking, thinking through a problem and coming up with solutions through discussion is a great method, almost like thinking aloud! But in other work areas, communication needs to be direct and purposeful.

- **Executive functioning.** Executive functioning is like the engine of the brain—it is the hub or control tower. It involves memory, attention, comprehension, decision-making, reactions to different situations, and the abilities to monitor, be adaptive, and be reflective. It helps with organization and application. There is a lot of evidence associating executive functioning difficulties with dyslexia.

- **Time management.** Adults with dyslexia tend to use the creative or visual areas of the brain. Direct and quick responses, organization, and planning are not normally features of visual creativity and innovation. As a result, time protocols not only are difficult to adhere to but also do not get the same cognitive priority as other aspects, such as creating something new.

- **Lack of attention to detail.** Adults with dyslexia tend to take a global perspective when problem-solving and also when reading. This means they can be excellent at grasping the big picture but perhaps not so great with the small details. It's important to appreciate that acquiring the big picture is a strength, and not everyone can do it!

- **Low self-esteem and reduced self-confidence.** Many people with dyslexia have experienced some form of failure—usually at school. Experiencing failure or even comparing yourself unfavorably with others in your peer group can lead to low self-esteem and reduced self-confidence. Low self-esteem can start when you are young and at school and persist into adulthood. The adult with dyslexia may be less confident and less willing to take risks in learning and in their daily work. They may be less willing to volunteer suggestions or ideas. Low self-esteem and reduced self-confidence can spill into other areas, including family life and social life. Low self-esteem and other factors, such as work overload, work challenges, and issues relating to social experiences and home life, can all in some way contribute to stress.

MY CHALLENGES

Write down all the obstacles you have faced and perhaps still are facing. Indicate their severity on a scale of 1 to 5, with 1 being mild and 5 being severe.

ELEMENTARY SCHOOL	HIGH SCHOOL/ COLLEGE	HOME	WORK
EXAMPLE: reading (3)			

Select four of the obstacles you listed and jot down how you have tried to overcome them. This can be quite revealing and can show you what you have achieved and how you did it. It can also show you the areas that you still need to work on.

OBSTACLE	STRATEGY

Some of the challenges you have noted or are aware of may be specific to your time at school, but many will likely be current and specific to you as an adult. Often the obstacles experienced by adults differ from those experienced by children. As an adult, your resilience can be lowered, particularly if you have encountered obstacles without reaching real success as you define it.

The Strengths of Dyslexia

Dyslexia can be described as a *difference* in how information is processed. This means reading, spelling, and writing can be challenging. But differences can be beneficial, and different ways of processing information can amount to strengths. For example, you may have a visual, right-brained global processing style, and this is a gift in many situations.

It's important to recognize and respect the strengths of dyslexia.

- **Vivid imagination.** The global right-brained preference used by adults with dyslexia can mean they can often "see the unseen." This means their visual and imaginative skills can be more advanced than others'. These skills can be very useful in occupations such as advertising, construction, filmmaking, and many more. Being able to think outside the box can be useful for most occupations and essential for teamwork.

- **Curiosity.** The investigative skills of people with dyslexia can be outstanding because of their inclination toward curiosity—the need to find out! I am always struck when running seminars for adults with dyslexia at the predominance of *why* questions. They indicate a search for answers and often include questions I'd never considered.

- **Intuition and insights.** Many of us operate on insights and intuition without realizing it. It's often these intuitive thoughts that guide our actions. The brain compensates for weaker areas all the time by using its stronger areas, so having a weaker left hemisphere can result in the adaptation of other parts of the brain, such as the visual and sensory areas. It's not surprising that people with dyslexia can have a heightened sensitivity and become more in tune with what others are thinking and what feels right.

- **Three-dimensional and spatial awareness.** When I'm assessing adults with dyslexia, invariably I note their superior visual-spatial skills. I'm usually not surprised when they remark that they are architects or engineers. People with dyslexia often think in a three-dimensional way.

- **Highly aware of the environment.** The work environment or the learning environment needs careful thought and attention. Some work environments can be more suited to the dyslexic adult than others. Usually people with dyslexia prefer an informal and open type of environment rather than a formal and restrictive one. They prefer an environment that is characterized by color and design rather than uniformity and regulation, and they can be very sensitive to their environment. For that reason, it is important to get it right!

- **Think in pictures rather than words.** For some people with dyslexia, words represent symbols, but pictures represent meaning. Combining pictures and words would be the perfect match, but it's unlikely that words alone can do the trick. We are fortunate in this respect, as more emphasis has been placed on visual types of learning. Schools and workplaces are now using videos as a serious learning tool, which helps learners think in pictures. In the workplace, when a manager is giving instructions while speaking to an employee who has dyslexia, that employee is drawing pictures in their mind of what they must do. People with dyslexia can become very adept at this skill, but it's important to appreciate that it's a different form of communication. Drawing pictures in your mind takes more time and attention than listening to words.

Workplace Considerations

In the workplace, adults with dyslexia often face a number of challenges, such as time management, organization, carrying out precise instructions, focusing on one task for an extended period, and remembering the sequence of a work activity. Here are some tips for dealing with these obstacles:

- **Structure your day.** Break your day into segments based on time or tasks. The secret is not to be too ambitious. It's too easy to try to cram a lot into a time segment, but that plan can hit a wall if you get an unexpected phone call or someone drops in to talk to you. Once you finish each segment or task, tick it off. If there are any unfinished tasks, include them in a separate list for either the end of the day or the next day. It's a good idea if you are working in time segments to leave a free space in the last segment for rollovers—tasks you were not able to complete in the time allocated so you are rolling them over.

- **Focus on one task.** This can be problematic as we are clearly living in an age of multitasking. It's a good idea to get "head space." You can do this by clearing everything from your head except the one task.

- **Plan extra time.** This is important, particularly if the task involves reading, but other tasks may also require more time. Try to add an extra 25 percent to the time you think the task will take. Remember that you will need time for checking and reviewing your work. Think in terms of time to accomplish the task, plus time to review it. Try to make this a habit.

- **Work on your reading.** Usually people with dyslexia will need more time for reading, so it is a good idea to work on speeding up your reading without too much pressure. One way of doing this is to read something you have read before, perhaps a novel or a news story. The story and the words will be familiar, so you should be able to read it faster.

- **Computer settings and applications.** Computers are a great asset to the adult with dyslexia. Try to make the most of this and adjust the settings, particularly the screen color and contrast. Determine what's best for you. It might be a good idea to make the screen less bright. Computer programs that offer text to speech have additional functionalities that can change the speed, voice, and accent. It's also possible for the application to highlight words and change background colors. Apps are available to allow speech to text, and this can be extremely helpful, particularly if you have difficulty producing written work quickly. It's now also possible to customize software for the individual user.

- **Charts and diagrams.** If you have to give a presentation or write a report, you may want to start with a diagram. This can help you generate your ideas and organize these into a coherent framework. Charts are another good choice because they require only a few words or short sentences to explain concepts.

- **Master the vocabulary of your industry.** All industries have their own language, and your job will be easier if you familiarize yourself with the language of your work. For example, if you're working in a car dealership, learn words such as *franchise*, *greenhouse gases*, and *gross margin*. It's a good idea to jot down these words and their definitions in your own personal notebook.

- **Lighting.** If you're working in an office or anywhere inside, lighting is important. It can have an impact on your ability to maintain your focus on a task. People with dyslexia often prefer low lighting rather than bright fluorescent lighting as softer light can reduce distractions, minimize glare, and help with focusing. You may find it helpful to have a small table light on your desk rather than a bright overhead light.

BUILDING UPON WORKPLACE STRATEGIES

Best for: self-knowledge and developing strengths

The exercise can help you become more adaptable to different situations at work and use your strengths more fully.

One of the differences between adults with dyslexia and children with dyslexia is that adults usually, through experience, have tried-and-tested strategies to call on. They may know what works for them and what doesn't. But at the same time, they have to be adaptable. Particularly in a workplace, demands change, colleagues move on, and new people—perhaps supervisors with differing management styles—move in. This adaptability can be seen as a coping strategy and, with experience, adults can become more familiar and more competent at recognizing and using this strategy.

INSTRUCTIONS: Part 1. Think of some of the workplace demands and obstacles you are currently experiencing or had when you first started your job. Jot them down along with your coping strategy.

OBSTACLE	STRATEGY

INSTRUCTIONS: Part 2. Take a moment to think about the answers you provided. What areas do you still want to work on? What coping strategies have been successful for you? What strengths do they show?

_____

_____

_____

_____

_____

Positive Psychology

Professors Rod Nicolson and Angela Fawcett use the concept of positive psychology with reference to dyslexia. They combine workplace strengths, cognitive strengths, and social strengths and suggest that these can help to change the perception of dyslexia from a negative to a positive trait. They suggest that adults with dyslexia have or can acquire work strengths such as resilience, proactivity, perseverance, and flexible coping; cognitive strengths such as creativity and visualization; and social strengths such as teamwork, empathy, and communication skills. Perhaps insightfulness can be included, as well.

An example of how someone with dyslexia would use some of these attributes is in learning how to use a new piece of software. Oftentimes, pages of instructions accompany the software, which can make it difficult for those with dyslexia if they have reading challenges. Through perseverance, however, they can master the material.

Reflect on how you might have used some of those attributes in your work. Consider this example: "In my job as an administrator, I had to use a new piece of software to help with planning and scheduling. I found it difficult at first but persevered until I mastered it at last. Perhaps it took me longer than some of my colleagues, but the important point is that I did it!"

The research does indicate that overlearning is necessary for people with dyslexia, and they will need repetition and more time to consolidate new learning. Don't worry if it takes you longer than someone else!

Career Choice

Career choice is a very important and sometimes overlooked point, as you may have been totally overjoyed purely at acquiring employment. I recall running a seminar for a group of adults with dyslexia and noting the diversity in occupations. Although some occupations may lend themselves more readily to the dyslexic person, there is no occupation that is out of reach for someone with dyslexia.

For example, professions that use visual and spatial skills and creativity, such as engineering or advertising, are excellent for many people with dyslexia. Other professions, such as librarian or newspaper editor, may not be a natural fit. But remember, people are adaptable, and those with dyslexia become quite adept at adapting!

A great example is architect Aidan Ridyard. In his piece "Reflecting on a Life with Dyslexia," Ridyard describes how he entered architectural college with no artistic training or ability to draw. He attributes his success to determination and adaptation skills—finding his own way to draw—and, of course, the increasing confidence that came with those skills. He suggests that the overriding lesson of his professional life has been understanding why he fails, learning how to sidestep the problem, and realigning the challenge with his own skills.

While some professions are better matches than others for people with dyslexia, if you implement strategies and accommodations, all occupations are possibilities.

THE A-LIST

There are many superb role models who have successfully used strategies to overcome the obstacles of dyslexia and who embody the unique strengths of dyslexia. This is beautifully documented in Tom West's book *In the Mind's Eye* and his follow-up, *Thinking Like Einstein*. West has conducted rigorous and exhaustive original research looking at key historical figures who believed they were dyslexic.

Many of these people relied on visual thinking and thinking outside the box. West cites the well-known case of Albert Einstein, as well as Thomas Edison, Winston Churchill, and Lewis Carroll, who all had dyslexia. All had to shift from linear thinking to creative thinking. Instead of replicating and extending the current conventions and knowledge base, they sought new answers to problems, often amid opposition from competitors and society at the time. These people are dyslexia heroes.

In the modern era, we have dyslexics like creative entrepreneur Richard Branson and film producer Guy Ritchie. We have actors like Henry Winkler and celebrity chefs such as Jamie Oliver. All of these people have displayed originality and creativity in their professions.

The annual conference for the International Dyslexia Association always spotlights a number of successful dyslexic adults, who recount their obstacles and how they overcame them. In 2019, one such person was John Hoke, Nike's chief design officer. Hoke showed how his dyslexia helped him develop innovative designs and also helped him foster and encourage teamwork and help others harness their skills and believe in themselves. Similarly, Sir Jackie Stewart—three-time world racing champion who was diagnosed as dyslexic at the age of 42—has talked about how dyslexia helped him in pursuit and perseverance of his ambitions, although in no way does he underplay the obstacles. The key message is that those obstacles can be overcome.

Thriving with Dyslexia

I hope this chapter has encouraged you to think positively about your dyslexia. It's good to be able to identify your strengths. You may not even be aware of them. One of the purposes of this book is to try to highlight your strengths through the tasks and activities.

The positive message in this chapter should also offer encouragement that with determination and practice, you can achieve what you want to achieve.

I want you to value your unique set of skills, your compassion and empathy, and your value to employers and the workplace, whatever occupation you are in. Most important, I want you to value yourself. The work you do in this book will help you achieve that.

The remainder of this book will offer a range of exercises that specifically focus on dyslexia. There will also be a host of tips and strategies that you can relate to your current work and personal life and also keep as a reference for the future.

CHAPTER TWO

IMPROVING LITERACY SKILLS

One of the important things I've discovered in my profession and considered throughout my career is that it's never too late to learn! This particularly applies to adults with dyslexia. Like everything you do—the more you practice, the better you become, whether you're learning to swim or building reading skills. Professional football players are very good at their sport, but they still have to practice, usually every day, and if they have a few days off, they usually feel it when they return. The secret is to keep reading! It does not matter what you read—newspapers, magazines, novels, comics, or movie subtitles. All these can help build reading skills, reading fluency, and confidence in reading.

This chapter will cover some of the main literacy obstacles adults with dyslexia face. Then it will present several exercises that focus on five important aspects of reading to help you address your challenges and build literacy skills.

Literacy Obstacles

The literacy challenges adults with dyslexia experience can vary depending on the individual. Generally speaking, some of the following points are common to most adults with dyslexia:

- **Difficulties in reading accuracy.** The person may not have full competence in the foundations of reading or decoding skills, and they may rely a great deal on context.

- **Speed-of-reading difficulties.** If someone is not familiar with rules of reading and not able to use reading strategies, they have to decode each unknown word.

- **Reluctance to read.** People with dyslexia may have difficulty transferring the print into visual pictures quickly and be easily distracted, which makes reading take a long time.

- **Need to reread text.** People with dyslexia have to read for accuracy and read again, perhaps many times, for comprehension.

- **Noting inferences in texts.** This is important for comprehension, but people with dyslexia are inclined to read literally and may miss the hidden meanings in a passage.

- **Difficulty with technical words.** Often technical words are not common, so learners will not have been exposed to these industry-specific words. Many of these unfamiliar words can look or sound similar.

- **Difficulty with proofreading.** Proofreading for many people can be challenging, as people are inclined to read for meaning.

- **Difficulty reading aloud.** Reading aloud is quite different from silent reading, particularly as it involves articulation. This can be challenging, and it is more difficult to skim a word when you're reading aloud. Adults with dyslexia should try to read silently.

- **Persistent spelling errors.** Many people with dyslexia have acquired bad spelling habits, and these have become ingrained and difficult to extinguish.

- **Difficulty with spelling rules.** This can be due to memory difficulties and reliance on spellcheckers.

- **Difficulty with grammatical structure.** In written work, the adult with dyslexia is often more preoccupied with just getting the job done. Grammatical structure needs to be a follow-up to the written work and can be part of the review of work.

- **Difficulty with sequencing.** For adults with dyslexia, ideas often just mingle with one another. Organizing and sequencing ideas can be difficult for people with dyslexia.

- **Difficulty identifying main points.** This is important for reading and writing. When writing, people with dyslexia can have difficulty identifying the key issues and may go off on a tangent. This can apply to any writing—whether a personal note or a report on something they've read.

- **Planning written work.** Writing is usually a linear process, and people with dyslexia think laterally. This can cause problems because the sequence of the written work may be difficult to follow. To help deal with this, people with dyslexia can start with a broad diagram (lateral thinking) and then discuss it in order to convert it into a linear sequential plan.

- **Attention span.** All the literacy activities, including reading, spelling, and writing, require people to pay attention. The research shows that people with dyslexia need more time to read and require overlearning to consolidate information. They may not be able to read some words automatically. This means attention needs to be constant and consistent.

Skill-Building: Orton-Gillingham Approach

The Orton-Gillingham approach (also called the O-G Multisensory Structured Language Approach to Teaching Literary Skills) is a well-established skill-building approach that is recognized as incorporating the five main elements of reading: phonological and phonemic awareness, phonics, fluency, vocabulary, and comprehension. It is widely used in schools in the United States and Canada, and it is also used for adults with literacy challenges. There are many variations of this approach, and a number of very popular packaged programs are widely available. (See the Resources section at the end of this book for a description of some of the most popular ones.) The National Reading Panel, which published a federally commissioned analysis of the rigorous research on reading, produced a detailed report that has been upheld by most in the field and is followed closely in the development and implementation of reading programs. The panel opted for five key areas in the teaching and acquiring of efficient reading skills in order to read proficiently.

- **Phonological awareness.** Recognizing individual sounds and sound combinations in words.

- **Phonics.** Recognizing the letters and letter combinations that make sounds and matching the visual symbols (letters) to the sounds. This is important for spelling.

- **Fluency.** Being able to read without too many hesitations or skipping words. This is important for comprehension.

- **Vocabulary.** This is often an issue with adults with dyslexia if they have not assimilated a working vocabulary, so reading is not automatic. This means they have to stop when they come across an unknown word. This has an impact on comprehension.

- **Comprehension.** This provides a purpose for reading and includes both literal comprehension and inferential comprehension (i.e., reading between the lines).

This chapter includes Orton-Gillingham–based activities that you can carry out either on your own or with a group. The activities are divided into the five key aspects of reading, but in no way do they represent a comprehensive literacy curriculum for those with dyslexia. They are meant to help you address some of the literacy obstacles you may be confronting. Not every activity will relate to the challenges you may be experiencing as an adult with dyslexia. Choose those that apply to the literacy skills you most want to improve.

Phonological Awareness and Phonics Activities

Phonological awareness and phonics is the ability to hear and manipulate larger units of sound, such as the beginnings and ends of words and syllables. *Phonemic awareness* is a subset of phonological awareness and is the ability to hear and manipulate individual phonemes (distinct, individual sounds). There is usually a crucial time for teaching phonological awareness and phonics, which normally occurs when children are very young. Some adults, however, still have some issues with this, and difficulties in matching the sounds to the visual images (individual letters or groups of letters) can impact reading and spelling.

Listening to rhymes and practicing using rhyming words can help develop awareness of sounds. Hearing the word and seeing it printed at the same time can also aid in developing awareness of the different sounds that make up a word. Using subtitles when watching a television program can be helpful as you can see the words and hear them at the same time.

Many of the successful reading approaches used in schools are based on acquiring efficient sound–symbol correspondence, but this is one of the areas of difficulty experienced by children with dyslexia. It's a barrier that can persist into adulthood.

The International Literacy Association claims that "teaching students the basic letter-sound combinations gives them access to sounding out approximately 84% of the words in English print." In addition to having an impact on reading, difficulties with phonics will also impact spelling. A number of activities in the chapter, therefore, will focus on spelling.

Following are several exercises that will help with phonological awareness and phonics.

RECIPE FOR SPELLING

Best for: identifying types of letters and letter combinations

This exercise will help you identify the different spelling patterns in words.

Spelling can be confusing for people with dyslexia because they may be unsure of how many letters represent a sound and unfamiliar with certain letter combinations and their purpose.

Let's review from the basic to the more complex so you can see different letter combinations and feel more confident when using them for your own spelling.

- There are 26 letters in the alphabet.

- *a, e, i, o,* and *u* are vowels. Every word requires a vowel in order to be a word. Sometimes vowels work together as a team to make one sound: *ou, ai, ay, ee, ea, oi, ow, oy*. These are considered one spelling, but two vowels are making the spelling.

- Sometimes *y* is referred to as a vowel because it can make the long *i* sound or the long e sound.

- When a vowel comes immediately before an r, it is referred to as an r-controlled vowel, as the two letters represent one spelling unit: *ar, er, ir, or, ur,* and *yr*.

- All letters that are not vowels are consonants. Consonants can work on their own, or they can come in combinations.

- One of the most common ways to see consonants is as a cluster, such as spr, str, and spl. They blend together easily, but you can hear all of the sounds.

- Other times, consonants work together, but they make only one sound or represent one letter unit, such as sh, th, wh, ch, tch, and ck.

INSTRUCTIONS: In the following ingredient list, identify and draw a line for all the spelling sounds you find in a word. I've provided some examples to get you started. For example, *jam* has three sounds: *j* and *a* and *m*. In this example, every letter makes a sound. On the other hand, using the word *beets*, we can see *ee* makes one sound, and in *radish*, *sh* makes one sound. Look at the following words and divide them into sounds with lines. Your spelling will improve as you get to know the combinations of letters that make specific sounds. The Answer Key begins on page 169.

j/a/m	b/ee/t/s	r/a/d/i/sh	k/e/l/p	b/r/ea/d
salt	meat	garlic	basil	
ham	nuts	mango	lemon	
cream	sprouts	shrimp	mushroom	
peas	ginger	seeds	oil	
milk	yeast	corn	miso	
fish	blueberry	almond	walnut	
broth	honey	celery	greens	

SPOT THE VOWEL

Best for: recognizing short and long vowel words

This exercise will help you with spelling and distinguishing between different types of vowels. This is important for recognizing spelling patterns.

It's important to recognize whether a vowel is short or long, as this will determine the reading or spelling of that word. A short vowel is closed in by one or two consonants at the end of a word.

For example, in the words *bag* and *cat*, the vowel *a* is short, as it is followed by a consonant.

Compare this with a vowel or consonant plus a long syllable, such as in the words *bike* and *tape*. The vowel sound is long. Similarly, the words *me*, *hi*, and *so* have long vowels, as there is no consonant closing them in at the end.

INSTRUCTIONS: Sort the following words into the proper column depending on whether they have a short vowel or a long vowel. The first one is done for you as an example.

WORDS	SHORT VOWEL	LONG VOWEL
grape		*grape*
mat		
pen		
go		
blend		
text		
bee		
sea		
prep		
shake		
cry		
trend		

SPELLING: DROP THE *E*

Best for: knowing how to properly spell words with suffixes

This exercise will give you practice at recognizing when to drop the *e* in suffixes It will also help you understand the rules that govern this spelling pattern.

A suffix is a letter or group of letters added to the end of a word that alters its meaning or grammatical function. Examples of suffixes include -tion, -ity, -er, -ness, -ism, -ment, -age, -able, and -ery. If a suffix starts with a vowel, the rule is to drop the *e* in the root word before adding the suffix. For example, *achieve* becomes *achievable* because the suffix -able starts with the vowel *a*. But if the suffix starts with a consonant, the rule is to keep the *e*. For example, *achieve* becomes *achievement* because the suffix -ment begins with the consonant *m*.

INSTRUCTIONS: For the following words, add the correct suffix (-*able*, -*ed*, -*ful*, -*ing*, -*less*, -*ment*), making sure to apply the proper rule about the *e* so the word is spelled correctly. Note that the words can take more than one suffix. The first one is done for you as an example.

hope	*hoped, hopeful, hoping, hopeless*
drive	
spike	
shame	
skate	
save	
strive	
state	
postpone	
bake	
fake	
brave	

TRICKY SPELLING

Best for: developing personal memory aids for tricky spellings

This activity will help you develop your own strategies for spelling tricky words. By doing this you are more likely to remember the strategy and the correct spelling.

Certain words are typically considered difficult for people with dyslexia and often have to be remembered by sight or using mnemonics. A mnemonic is a simple technique that uses association between two things to help with memory.

INSTRUCTIONS: Give yourself three days to learn how to spell each word and remember it. For example, memory aids for the words *because* and *friend* are provided in the following table.

WORD	MAKE YOUR OWN MEMORY AID
because	*Big elephants can always use some exercise.*
awkward	
auxiliary	
achieve	
beige	
caress	
conceit	
debris	
embarrass	
foreign	
friend	*Friday is at the end of the week.*

LIST IT: SPELLING CHOICES

Best for: developing sound–symbol correspondence

This exercise will provide you with practice using some other spelling rules and help you match sounds with letters.

Here are some clues to help you:

- **ay:** usually at end of word

- **ck:** after short vowel, never at beginning of word

- **tch:** after short vowel, never at beginning of word

- **dge:** after short vowel, never at beginning of word

INSTRUCTIONS: Complete the columns in the following table as noted. The first few are done for you as examples.

/ā/ spelled ay, ai, a_e, and a	/ch/ spelled ch and tch	/k/ spelled k, ck, and c	/f/ spelled ph and f	/j/ spelled dge	/ī/ spelled i, y, and i_e
List at least two more words that use these spellings.	List at least four more words that use these spellings.	List at least two more words that use each of these spellings.	List at least four more words that use these spellings.	List at least five more words that use this spelling.	List at least three more words that use these spellings.
play	coach	king	graph	judge	fly
rain	catch	duck	first		strive
brave		camp			

POSITIONAL SPELLINGS

Best for: recognizing that certain spelling choices are heavily dependent on where you find them in a word

This activity will help you become more familiar with the spelling of challenging words that are often misspelled by adults with dyslexia.

Certain spellings are associated with certain positions in a word. Following are some common letters and letter groupings and where they typically fall in a word.

INSTRUCTIONS: Part 1. Think of a word for each spelling. The first one is done for you as an example.

dge: after a short vowel, usually at end of word

dodge

j: at beginning of word, never at end

ch: beginning or end position (but not after a short vowel)

tch: after short vowel at end of word

ay: end of word

ai: middle spelling, usually with *l* or *n*

_____

a_e: middle spelling

_____

i_e: middle spelling

_____

y: end spelling

_____

c: beginning; with the letters *a*, *o*, *u*; blends with consonants *l*, *r*

_____

k: beginning; with the letters *i*, *e*, and long vowels

_____

ck: after short vowel, usually at end of word

_____

INSTRUCTIONS: Part 2. For the following constructions, fill in the correct letters or letter groupings depending on their position in the word. The first two are done for you as examples.

nail (*ai, ay*)	cr__(*y, i_e*)	__ilt (*k, c*)	___ing (*c, k*)
camp (*c, k, ck*)	fl___(*y, i_e*)	pr___(*ay, ai*)	____imp (*tch, ch*)
sna___(*k, ck*)	p___n (*ay, ai*)	h_____(*ay, a_e*)	sp__k__(*y, i_e*)
str___(*ay, ai*)	tru___(*k, ck*)	fle___(*ck, k*)	____ick (*tch, ch*)
cru___(*tch, ch*)	ca__(*tch, ch*)	li__(*ck, k*)	sn____l (*a_e, ai*)
__unk (*j, dge*)	do____(*dge, j*)	___air (*ch, tch*)	clo__(*ck, k*)
fri___(*dge, j*)	b__k__(*a_e, ay*)	b__k__(*ai, a_e*)	bla___(*ck, c*)

PLURALS: RULES AND EXCEPTIONS

Best for: making words plural considering rules and exceptions

Plurals are used a great deal, and this exercise will give you practice using plurals and noting which types of plurals are used and why.

When making words plural, there are three rules.

- A singular noun names one person, place, thing, or idea, while a plural noun names more than one person, place, thing, or idea.

- Most singular nouns need an *s* at the end to become plural. For example, the plural of *book* is *books*, the plural of *table* is *tables*, and the plural of *chair* is *chairs*.

- Singular nouns ending in s, ss, x, z, zz, sh, ch, and tch need an -es at the end to become plural. For example, the plural of *bus* is *buses*, the plural of *cross* is *crosses*, the plural of *box* is *boxes*, the plural of *church* is *churches*, and the plural of *inch* is *inches*.

However, there are exceptions to these rules:

- Some nouns are the same in both singular and plural. Examples are *deer*, *sheep*, and *series*.

- Some nouns ending in *f* require you to change the *f* to a *v* and add -es to make them plural. For example, the plural of *elf* is *elves*, the plural of *calf* is *calves*, and the plural of *loaf* is *loaves*.

- Nouns ending in *y* often require you to change the *y* to an *i* and then add -es to make them plural. For example, the plural of *baby* is *babies*. The exception to this is if a noun ends in *y* and a vowel precedes the *y*. In that case, add *s* at the end to make it plural. For example, the plural of *toy* is *toys*.

INSTRUCTIONS: Use the rules to make the following words plural.

church	
box	
key	
way	
loss	
dish	
fly	
dress	
piano	
fish	

WORD PLAY: SOUNDS THE SAME

Best for: developing familiarity of words with different spellings that sound the same

This exercise will help you practice the spellings of different words that sound the same. This can be confusing, and practice is the best way to achieve competence.

There are a host of words that sound the same but are spelled differently and have different meanings. These are called homophones. Although English may appear to have a highly complex spelling system, if you know the rules and where a word is derived from, you'll be able to recognize spellings and make the best choices. For example, English makes use of Latin roots, Greek roots, and French and early Anglo-Saxon influences. That explains why there are many different rules and exceptions to rules, and it also accounts for the spelling challenges you may experience.

Words that sound the same but are spelled differently are called *homophones*. Among the most common homophones are *their* and *there*. Quite often you have to just try to remember these and use them correctly—eventually you will know by looking at them if they are correct. You can use a memory trick (mnemonic) and say the word *their* has an *i* and that refers to people (*their books*), while *there* has an *e* and that refers to the environment or position (*over there*). It's best if you make up your own tricks and strategies for the homophones you often use. Some general examples are shown in the following table.

WORD	EXAMPLE	WORD	EXAMPLE
their	their books	there	over there
sea	water	see	eyesight
too	also	two	number
ale	beer	ail	unwell
allowed	give permission	aloud	speak out
air	atmosphere	heir	a successor

INSTRUCTIONS: Find some words of your own that sound the same but are spelled differently. Try to find words that you would likely use in your workplace or elsewhere. Then fill out the table. Doing this will help you remember the words so you can choose the right homophone when you're writing.

WORD	EXAMPLE	WORD	EXAMPLE

Fluency Activities

Reading fluency is the ability to read accurately, smoothly, and with expression. Adults with dyslexia tend to hesitate while reading because they may come across an unknown word or lose focus, either visually or in comprehension. If the flow of the reading is interrupted, it will have an impact on fluency and, therefore, on comprehension as well.

When you're reading a book, it's a good idea to read and listen to the book at the same time. You can apply this technique to electronic reading such as on a computer, laptop, or any mobile device. It can help with pronunciation and word recognition, and these factors will promote fluency. We are fortunate that technology is on our side, and it continues to become increasingly more sophisticated. A number of websites offer text to speech so you can listen and read along. Do a search for "free text-to-speech" and you'll find several!

If you are part of a small group or support circle, working on a drama production can also be useful. Each person reads the same lines over and over in order to remember them, and this type of repetition can help with fluency. It can also help build vocabulary. There is no doubt that knowledge of vocabulary can help with fluency. But the most important thing is *automaticity*, that is, being able to recognize words automatically. This is achieved by overlearning, and that is why drama—remembering specific lines and being able to read them with full meaning and expression—is helpful.

Following are some general tips to increase reading fluency:

- **Avoid focusing on every word**. Instead, look at groups of two to four words. In the first sentence, I zeroed in on the words *avoid focusing* and *every word*.

- **Develop your vocabulary**. This is very important in order to achieve automaticity, and it helps with fluency.

- **Practice**. Read anything and everything. There are words around you everywhere you go—advertising, signs, online content, and more! Try to watch movies or TV programs with subtitles on.

- **Ask yourself questions while reading**. Why are you reading this, what is happening, what do you want to find out, and what sparked your interest in reading it? This will give you a system for approaching text you are reading.

- **Try reading something you have read before and are extremely familiar with.** Utilize skimming and scanning. This will increase your reading speed but also give you practice at reading quickly.

- **Pace yourself.** It's good to read for even just five to 10 minutes a day. You can gradually extend the time. The important thing is to practice.

The following are several strategies that will help with fluency.

DAILY FIX: RAPID WORD RECOGNITION

Best for: achieving automaticity in reading tricky words

This exercise will give you practice in reading fluently, particularly those tricky words that can disrupt fluency.

It's important to achieve automaticity and be able to read challenging words automatically.

INSTRUCTIONS: For each day of the month, select one challenging word you have come across in your workplace or in your personal reading.

1. Create a table with boxes for each of the words.

2. Read one word a day, a number of times throughout the day, so that by the end of the day you can read it automatically.

3. At the end of the week, read all seven words in a row a number of times until you have achieved automaticity.

4. To consolidate this for the following week, in addition to reading new words, you can also read the previous week's words in reverse order just to make sure you are not reading by remembering the sequence of the words.

5. Do this every day for the month; then you can start a new 30- or 31-day word table.

The following example includes words a mechanic would encounter, as well as some words from newspaper articles.

mechanical	ingenious	laborious	craftsman
workbench	technical	polytechnics	apprentice
engine	horsepower	cylinder	acceleration
electric	business	rotation	turbocharger
combustion	cooler	eroded	windshield
accelerator	compartment	odometer	ignition
manifold	catalytic	alternator	decompressor
periodical	current	innovation	

SKIM IT

Best for: developing reading speed

This exercise will give you practice at speed-reading and help you identify the important words in a text.

Skimming is a very useful strategy for people with dyslexia. It can help you identify the key words and build comprehension and fluency. This speed-reading strategy helps you read material very rapidly without having to read every word. The purpose is to get the main ideas so you comprehend the information. You can then determine if it's important enough to read it again.

When using skimming to read a book, a good tip is to first read the jacket and inside cover carefully without skimming, as this will give you a context for the book, the main characters, and something about the plot.

The following passage is taken from the introduction to this section, and you will note that I have bolded some of the key words. Just by reading these key words, you can get a general idea of what the passage is about.

Reading **fluency** is the ability to **read accurately, smoothly**, and with **expression**. Adults with dyslexia tend to **hesitate while reading because** they may come across an **unknown word** or lose focus, either visually or in comprehension. If the flow of the reading is interrupted, it will have an impact on fluency and, therefore, comprehension as well.

INSTRUCTIONS: Take a piece of text you are working on, perhaps a page from a book. After reading it a few times, underline or bold the key words. This can be your reference. When you look at that text again, you only need to read those key words.

SCAN AND HAVE FUN

Best for: spotting key words in text, developing reading speed

This activity will help you decide if the text is going to be useful for you and if you should read it all.

Scanning can accompany skimming, although they serve slightly different purposes. While skimming helps you read faster to get the general idea of the passage, scanning helps you find an important piece of information without having to read the whole text.

Usually, you'll know what you are looking for. For example, if you're reading a report on a new product, you may scan to the reviews of the product or to the price. These factors may determine whether it's worthwhile to read more about this product. Scanning can help with fluency, as it allows you to get information quicker. It also can help with comprehension because you obtain specific insights into what you're reading.

Scanning is best practiced using the following sequence:

1. Have some background knowledge about what you are about to read.

2. Have an idea of the key points you need to know.

3. Move your eyes quickly across each line.

4. Make sure you pay attention to the first sentence of each paragraph and any headings or subheadings.

5. If you spot something important, note it with a check mark or highlight the line.

6. Once you have completed scanning the material, ask yourself if you have the information you were looking for.

7. Note what you have obtained from the scan and what you still need to know.

You use scanning sometimes without realizing it—for example, when you are perusing websites or a television guide. Eventually you will find that you can become quite proficient at scanning, and together with skimming, it can increase your reading speed and comprehension.

INSTRUCTIONS: Try the strategy of scanning with a work manual or a nonfiction book. If you are studying, try it with some of the text you have to read for a course.

SIGHT WORD CARDS

Best for: developing reading fluency, working toward automaticity in word recognition, overlearning

This activity will help you develop automaticity in reading. This will help you read more fluently and prevent you from stopping to sound out difficult words.

Sight words don't follow regular phonetic patterns. You need to be able to read them by sight rather than by breaking them down into their phonetic components, Sight words need to be memorized. Examples of sight words include *apple*, *eye*, *their*, *have*, *egg*, and *horse*—you cannot spell them by sounding them out.

INSTRUCTIONS: Follow these steps.

1. Make a list of words that you come across in your workplace or elsewhere.

2. Determine whether the words you have listed are sight words.

3. Make flash cards for the sight words. Include the sight word in large letters and the meaning of the word under it in smaller letters.

4. Keep the flash cards on hand and select one or two every day to study. This will help with reading, spelling, vocabulary, and comprehension.

RECORDED READING AND OTHER TIPS FOR SPEED

Best for: developing confidence in reading, reading fluently with comprehension

This exercise will help you with reading comprehension as the recorded version will be read with expression.

Recording yourself reading different types of material and listening to the recordings is a good way to improve fluency and boost confidence. You should do this with both materials you're familiar with and can read fluently and with text you haven't read before.

INSTRUCTIONS: Record yourself reading a familiar text and a new one. Listen to the recordings. Compare the two and note how you can develop fluency with practice. Record the new passage a number of times until you are fluent. This underlines the point that practice is so important with reading.

Vocabulary Activities

Vocabulary is important in learning to read but also in reading to learn. Those who have difficulty reading are missing out on a great deal, and a limited vocabulary can have an impact on comprehension.

It takes the average learner about 25 experiences with a word before they "own" it in speech. This means that overlearning is important for acquiring and consolidating new vocabulary.

If you have access to someone who can read aloud to you, that can be helpful, particularly if you also have a copy of the text or book. That way, you can see the word and hear it at the same time. The accomplished reader will usually read fluently and place emphasis on key words, and this can also help with comprehension. The process of two people reading aloud together is called *paired reading*, which is also a good strategy for fluency. Before beginning paired reading, any unusual words should be defined with a number of examples. You can then try to say a sentence yourself using each new word.

The development of vocabulary has a significant impact on all the components of efficient and fluent reading. It helps with accuracy through word recognition and can also help with fluency, as the word will be familiar to you. Additionally, when vocabulary increases, comprehension of the text also increases.

Here are some general tips for developing your vocabulary.

* **Read.** Like everything, you need to practice to become efficient. This means read anything you can lay your hands—newspapers, magazines, and even the subtitles on TV.

- **Make notes of what you have read.** This is helpful if you want to build your vocabulary. Note new words; by writing them down, you will remember them better.

- **Have an inquiring mind.** Whenever you read or watch something, search for additional information on the topic, the people included, or anything else you may be interested in. If you have watched a good documentary, for example, go online and find out more about the people involved. This will help you practice reading in a way that can hold your interest.

The following exercises and strategies can help with vocabulary building.

SENTENCE STARTERS

Best for: developing a template for starting written or oral responses

This activity will give you more confidence in writing and help you get started with a writing exercise.

Quite often, adults with dyslexia have difficulty getting started with a piece of written work. This can apply to reports, notes, presentations, or any piece of writing, however short or long. But I find that once they start, they can then shape the response quite effectively and in their own way.

Following are some general prompts for answering emails. Even if you change the opener after getting started, I can assure you that it will help you with subsequent sentences.

- Thank you very much for responding to this email . . .

- I agree with this, but . . .

- That is a good idea. Can we perhaps also . . .

- I have read over this and think it will work well because . . .

- Can we also consider . . .

- Yes, I have already thought of that, and it is a good idea. Perhaps we can . . .

- Sorry for the delay in responding, but I wanted to check out a few points first . . .

- Things are going well here, and we seem to have turned a corner now . . .

INSTRUCTIONS: Now create your own sentence starters for emails or other situations. You can do this with your work or personal life in mind, based on what you do and the types of questions people often ask you. You can have the sample responses beside you as you begin. After a while, you'll be able to do this automatically!

_____

_____

_____

_____

_____

_____

OWN THAT WORD

Best for: extending and enriching your vocabulary

This activity will help you become familiar with new words and use them more frequently.

New words need to be consolidated, and the best way of doing that is to use the word as much as possible. This activity will encourage you to use the same word in two different sentences.

INSTRUCTIONS: Using the following list, try to use each word in a different position in a sentence, as this will further help you to own the word. For example, using the word *prefer*, you could say, "I would prefer to start this now." "If you prefer, we can do this together." The first one is done for you as an example.

client

As a client, your interests come first. The salesperson was happy about securing another client.

auxiliary

agenda

_____

estimate

_____

license

_____

unnecessary

_____

OWN THAT SENTENCE

Best for: developing interpretation of text, simplifying sentences

This exercise will help you understand some jargon and challenging phrases more easily. It will also help you put them into your own words.

You may hear or read a sentence that makes you say to yourself, "Well, what does that mean?" You then spend the next little while trying to figure it out. This activity will help you do that by providing you with some practice at rephrasing sentences to make them more easily understood.

INSTRUCTIONS: For each of the following sentences, create a simpler, more succinct alternative. You may want to use a thesaurus to help with this task. This exercise uses some words from the previous activity, which is a great way to practice overlearning.

1. My candid projection is that the current schedule is untenable.

_____

_____

2. I was quite frank in telling him the idea was superfluous and that the merchandise in question is redundant.

_____

_____

3. She was in a frenzy when the consumer projection was adjusted despite her endeavors.

_____

_____

4. The patron had a permit for the parking spot and was irate at being penalized for parking there.

_____

_____

5. The company made an endeavor to introduce specific contemporary ideas, but the lack of a license meant the initial proposal was untenable.

_____

_____

SENTENCES: SOUNDS THE SAME

Best for: using the correct version of words that have multiple meanings in a sentence

This activity will give you practice at distinguishing between similar-sounding words and will also help with spelling.

This is a follow-up to the "Word Play: Sounds the Same" activity, this time applying the concept to sentence structure.

INSTRUCTIONS: Each of the sentences has a word missing. Insert the correct word from the list provided.

buy	by
coarse	course
complement	compliment
genes	jeans
mail	male
peace	piece
raise	rays
right	write
stationary	stationery
too	two

1. Can you pick up the _____ today from the post office?

2. The study of _____ is well funded, as it can detect future illnesses.

3. If you want to remember this, _____ it down!

4. The larger kayak is for _____ people.

5. The shirt was on sale, so he wanted to _____ it.

6. The car at the red traffic signal was _____.

7. I gave the new client a _____ on his shoes.

8. The anthropology _____ at the university is challenging.

9. He switched off the radio to get some _____ and quiet.

10. My job had changed a lot, so I wanted a _____.

MAKE YOUR POINT

Best for: identifying key points in text, summarizing opinions

This activity will provide you with practice at getting your point across. This can be helpful for written work as well as for verbal discussions.

No matter where you work, you will likely need to express your thoughts to colleagues, management, clients, and customers.

There are a number of ways of doing this:

• Write in numbered or lettered lists or bullet points (as done here).

• Provide a point and follow it with an example.

• If writing prose, use effective transition words, such as *moreover*, *furthermore*, and *additionally*.

• Compare points so you can do an either/or scenario.

No matter how you choose to express yourself, it's a good idea to summarize everything at the end and allow for the recipient to get back to you with their thoughts. Each of these can be tricky, so you'll want to practice.

INSTRUCTIONS: Rewrite the following passage. Try to use the different formats in the preceding list to make this passage clearer to the reader.

Dyslexia and Culture

It can be suggested that teachers need to consult and collaborate with people who have a sound knowledge of the cultural background of students in order to avoid confusing common second language errors with indicators of dyslexia. These can overlap, as in the case of left-right confusion in Urdu, which is written from right to left, and with auditory discrimination with Punjabi speakers, who may have difficulty with p and b. It is important to consider information from parents or caregivers as they may have a more complete picture of their child in a range of settings, including those not involving language skills. Teachers may be alerted to a difficulty if the student has a lack of interest in books, good comprehension but low reading skills, and persistent problems in phonological awareness despite adequate exposure to English.

DESCRIBE THE ART

Best for: developing vocabulary, observation, creativity

This activity will help you develop your vocabulary and further help with reading and writing.

INSTRUCTIONS: Use the following general questions as prompts to describe the pictures you see.

1. What do the colors say to you?

2. What makes them eye-catching?

3. Do the pictures tell you anything about the artists?

4. Can you think of titles for these pieces?

5. If you were to describe them, what would your first sentence be?

_____

_____

_____

_____

_____

_____

As a follow-up, look at some pieces of art, including photography, in the area where you live, in your own home, or online.

Practice with these art examples using the same questions as prompts. You may want to add some of your own questions to the list.

DON'T SAY *SAID*

Best for: extending and varying vocabulary used in writing, understanding less-common words in reading

This activity will help you avoid using the same words repetitively and develop a range of alternative words to use.

There is a song by the Beatles titled "She Said She Said." Although the song is popular and very melodic, *said* must count among the most overused words in the English language.

You will find in your reading, particularly if you are reading a novel, that authors tend to use more descriptive alternatives, such as the following:

added	argued	asked
blurted	cautioned	declared
frowned	gasped	insisted
insisted	joked	muttered
ordered	retorted	roared
screamed	shouted	snapped
suggested	teased	whispered
yelled		

INSTRUCTIONS: Select 10 of the alternatives listed and create two sentences using each.

_____

_____

_____

_____

_____

_____

_____

Comprehension Activities

Some might argue that comprehension is the most important of the five factors in acquiring reading competency. Basically, if you're not able to comprehend, then you'll have little incentive to read.

There are many different aspects to comprehension, and some of those will be developed in the activities in this section.

Background knowledge is important, as is pre-reading discussion with others to gain insight. If the subject matter is familiar, it will be easier for the reader to comprehend.

As previously discussed, fluency is important for reading comprehension, as a fluent reader is able to read smoothly from one sentence to another. This helps the reader make meaningful connections between sentences. Additionally, if they still do not comprehend, they will likely use their background knowledge to help bring meaning to the sentence. This task is carried out very quickly by a competent and fluent reader. But it stands to reason that if there are any weaknesses in the reading chain, such as word identification, vocabulary, or fluency, then comprehension will be affected.

Competent readers will also interact with the text by asking themselves questions about what they're reading as they read, particularly if they come across an idea or concept that's new to them and causes them to reconsider their existing knowledge base.

In this section, you'll find activities focused on words and phrases and on using inferences. These are important for full reading comprehension.

DAY TIMER: WORD TRICKS

Best for: developing comprehension using words that have the same spelling but different meanings

This activity will help you develop your comprehension skills and learn the multiple meanings of some words. Here, we're focusing on comprehending the meaning of the words.

INSTRUCTIONS: Following are 15 words, each listed twice. Write down a definition for each word. It's okay to look up the definitions. The idea is to familiarize yourself with two meanings of a word that is spelled the same.

address	
address	
bear	
bear	
case	
case	
contract	
contract	
fine	
fine	
found	
found	
fudge	
fudge	

grouse	
grouse	
lead	
lead	
match	
match	
object	
object	
pound	
pound	
right	
right	
row	
row	
tender	
tender	

As a follow-up, think of words that are spelled the same but have different meanings that you use for work or in your everyday life or that you have trouble defining. Write them down in a notebook, along with the different definitions.

MATCHING THE PHRASES

Best for: practicing using meaningful phrases, developing a greater understanding of phrases

This exercise focuses on comprehension of phrases and will help you bring your language comprehension skills to a higher level.

This activity will help you comprehend the meaning of phrases that are related to one another. This is a challenging activity. Try to complete as many of the items as you can. You can always come back to it later.

INSTRUCTIONS: In the following table, match each statement to the statement it most relates to by writing the same number after it. See the examples marked number 1 in bold.

Democracy is viewed as beneficial 1	The work recreation room	Was the role of a key member of staff	Had many pages and took a long time to read
Time management	The work manual	As it helped him manage his finances	Reduce blood flow around the body
The kitchen was fully equipped	The study of genes	Should be free	Was canceled because of terrible weather
Sedentary occupations	**Since everyone is able to vote 1**	The work golf outing	Occupied lots of space in his work van
Overtime was helpful	Reading current work reports	She was rewarded by her employer	But knew what he was capable of
The medical journal	Public transportation	With fridge and microwave	For meeting her monthly goals
The large tool kit	Includes reviews of recent clinical studies	Listed job duties	Can detect the probability of health issues
The health and safety information manual	The swimmer faced a major challenge	Was used by most in their free time	Was important because her schedule was already overbooked

READ BETWEEN THE LINES

This exercise will help you look at the real meaning of a piece of text and read between the lines!

Adults with dyslexia, because they have challenges with reading, tend to read literally. They read and comprehend exactly what is on the page. As adults become proficient in reading, they can then apply their own interpretation of the words on the page, and that can be different from the actual word. This is called *inferential reading*. For example, the word *frown* implies scowling or being unhappy. But when we see it in the phrase *frowned with a slight smirk*, we understand there is a double or hidden meaning to the word *frown*.

It's important particularly when you're reading fiction to look for inferences. Inferences can be much more powerful than the meanings of the actual words. You as a reader are using clues provided by the author to obtain the real intended meaning. Following are some examples of inferences.

1. *The dog pushed the lounge door open, and the owner was shocked to see a newspaper in shreds scattered over the floor.*

   • The inference here is that the dog chewed the newspaper.

2. *The football fans exited the game early with sad, dour expressions.*

   • The inference here is that their team was losing badly.

INSTRUCTIONS: Create four inferences in phrases or sentences. After each inference, write your interpretation of it.

_____

_____

_____

_____

_____

_____

_____

_____

_____

_____

CATCHY PHRASES: IDIOMS

Best for: recognizing the meanings of common idioms, developing knowledge of idioms

This activity will help you become more aware of idioms, understand them, and be able to use them appropriately.

Idioms are words and phrases that are not meant to be taken literally. For full comprehension, idioms are important to understand, as they are used a great deal in speech and in writing. For example, _driving me up the wall_ has nothing to do with cars or walls. It means a person has had enough.

INSTRUCTIONS: Part 1. Following are four idioms. Write the meaning of each idiom.

at the drop of a hat

_____

call it a day

_____

under the weather

_____

loose cannon

_____

INSTRUCTIONS: Part 2. Write the idiom for each clue listed in the table.

This is a challenging activity. Try to write as many of the answers as possible. If you feel the activity is too challenging, sneak a peek at the answers at the back of the book. You can then look upon this as a knowledge-gaining exercise.

CLUE	IDIOM
very expensive	costs and arm and a leg
not want to decide	sit on the fence
idealistic	
what someone is thinking	
a disputed issue	
to come up to expectations	
exactly right	
choose between two unpleasant choices	
a problem to be avoided	
inexperienced, new to something	
familiar with the procedure	
when a situation becomes difficult	

LEVELS OF READING COMPREHENSION

Best for: appreciating different aspects to reading comprehension, recognizing different types of reading texts

This exercise will help you check that you have understood a passage and give you steps to follow to assist with comprehension.

There are different levels of reading depending on purpose and reasons for reading the text. You can read for basic understanding, and you can also read for critical reflection. Ideally this is what you want to achieve, but it depends on the purpose of the reading. The first thing to ask yourself is "What do I need to achieve from reading the text?" The levels of reading include:

LEVELS OF READING

- **Literal level.** Comprehending factual information such as who, what, why, where, when, and how.

- **Inferential level.** Comprehending inferences, that is, "reading between the lines." This would include questions such as "Why do you think he said that?" and "Did he really mean that?"

- **Creative level.** This would encourage originality and reflection. You can imagine your own ending to a story or a different use of an object, for example.

- **Critical level.** This encourages analysis and evaluation. Questions that can help with the critical level include "Did you enjoy the book? Why or why not?" and "What was confusing about the book?"

INSTRUCTIONS: Choose a piece of text and consider these different levels as you go through the text. You may want to jot down some thoughts and answers.

GUIDED READING QUESTIONS

Best for: asking the right questions after reading, developing and expanding comprehension of text, overlearning

This exercise will help you take your comprehension to the next level by giving you practice asking the most appropriate questions in order to develop comprehension.

Sometimes if the passage is complex you can lose track of what is being said. It's a good idea, therefore, to check that you're comprehending the passage as you read it and particularly at the end. This also helps you think about what you need to do to monitor and extend your comprehension.

INSTRUCTIONS: To further your abilities and improve reading comprehension, read a book or magazine article using the comprehension-monitoring steps in the process. Afterward, answer some or all of the following questions.

What did you learn?

_____

_____

What was difficult to understand?

_____

_____

What do you still need to know?

_____

_____

Can you note the difficult words?

_____

_____

How did you feel reading this?

_____

_____

Would you like to read more from this author? Why or why not?

_____

_____

Did you find the contents page helpful?

_____

_____

What changes do you suggest that would make the text better for you as someone with dyslexia?

_____

_____

CHAPTER THREE

BUILDING AUDITORY, VISUAL, AND SPATIAL SKILLS

This chapter will focus on auditory, visual, and spatial issues that people with dyslexia often experience. You'll engage in activities that can help you improve your skills in these areas. Also included will be memory and sequencing, both of which can be challenging for adults with dyslexia. (I'll also talk about memory in the following chapter on executive functioning.)

Auditory Aspects

Auditory processing and *auditory perception* are important elements in developing competence in reading. Auditory perception is how we receive sound, and auditory processing is how we understand what we hear. Both relate to *phonological awareness*, which is the awareness of sounds and is necessary for learning to read.

Auditory processing and auditory perception are very closely associated with dyslexia, and difficulties in these areas can result not only in reading challenges but also in difficulties in communication and carrying out instructions. Some of the factors associated with difficulties in auditory processing and perception include:

- **Auditory discrimination.** Distinguishing between separate and different sounds.

- **Auditory memory.** Recalling information that is spoken. This can be short term or long term.

- **Auditory sequencing.** Remembering and recalling the order of sounds and words and any information that is provided orally.

Visual Factors

Not all adults with dyslexia will have visual issues. Some people may even be strong visually, particularly for shapes and designs and perhaps colors, too. There is also a visual element in reading. Being strong visually can assist with scanning and skimming text, which help you increase your reading speed.

Some adults with dyslexia can experience visual disturbance when reading print, which can cause blurring, words merging, and omissions of words or lines. People with dyslexia sometimes find that colored overlays or colored backgrounds diminish visual disturbance. Large font sizes and additional spacing between lines can also help. I prefer to read when there is adequate spacing between lines. Lighting is also important. Some people with dyslexia can be sensitive to light, and this can cause issues when reading, particularly if the lighting is too strong and glaring. You can use visual filters, such as colored lenses or a glare filter on your computer screen, to help. These may also be effective in alleviating eyestrain when reading.

Spatial Awareness

Many adults with dyslexia have adequate, even exceptional, spatial awareness, but for some, this can be a significant weakness. In extreme cases, this can be associated with *dyspraxia*, which is a difficulty with coordination, balance, and awareness of the proximity of objects. Like dyslexia, dyspraxia is also seen on a continuum, and there can be an overlap between dyslexia and dyspraxia.

This chapter will provide exercises to help develop spatial awareness, and even if you think your spatial ability is fine, these can still be fun activities.

Auditory, visual, and spatial skills can be incorporated into the broader area of executive functioning, which will be further discussed in the next chapter. But it's important that these factors are also recognized independently and developed and improved through appropriate instruction. You'll find a variety of exercises throughout this chapter, and you can do them on your own or with another person. If you're part of a support group, the activities can be useful and fun to work through together. You can do them all or select the ones most appropriate for you.

As with all activities and exercises in this book, those in this chapter should be used as a learning tool and referred to for information and support. Some of the activities may not be directly relevant to you right now, but they may at a later date if you change careers or commence a college course. Remember, one person's dyslexic profile may be different from someone else's. But there are usually some common elements, and it's likely that the activities in this chapter will be of relevance to most adults with dyslexia.

Auditory Processing Activities

TONGUE TWISTERS

Best for: auditory discrimination, vocabulary, pronunciation, concentration

This activity will help you with articulation and developing your vocabulary.

Tongue twisters are good practice, as they have to be articulated properly to make sense. Often, they include *alliteration*, which is the occurrence of the same letter or the same sound in words that are next to or close to one another.

INSTRUCTIONS: Part 1. Practice the following tongue twisters. Start slowly and eventually build up speed as you repeat each of them a few times.

1. She sells seashells by the seashore.

2. A good cook could cook as many cookies as a good cook who could cook cookies.

3. How much wood would a woodchuck chuck if a woodchuck could chuck wood? A woodchuck would chuck all the wood he could chuck if a woodchuck could chuck wood.

While not easy, this is good practice for articulation and auditory discrimination. Sometimes when adults with dyslexia are at work meetings, they may mispronounce a word and feel embarrassed afterward. It's best to laugh off an occurrence like this. Almost everyone occasionally mispronounces words.

INSTRUCTIONS: Part 2. Practice the following tongue twisters each day as many times as you like. Time yourself and note your quickest time.

DAY	ALLITERATION	TIME
Monday	Seven sisters slept soundly on Sunday by the seashore.	
Tuesday	Fred's firefighter friend Frank found the firecrackers by the fireside.	
Wednesday	Frivolous Finnigan finished the funny fable first on Friday.	
Thursday	Quirky Quincy quickly and quietly snatched the quaint hat from Quinney in Quail Ridge Court in Quebec.	
Friday	Nick's naughty nephew needed nectarines, noodles, and nachos.	
Saturday	Sammy sometimes watched sports on Saturday and splattered himself silently over the sofa in a sweater and sandals.	

You can use Sunday to recap on what you have learned that week. As you practice, congratulate yourself as you gain speed while maintaining accuracy.

IS IT OR ISN'T IT?: COMMONLY CONFUSED WORDS

Best for: auditory discrimination, vocabulary, comprehension, confidence

This exercise will help with comprehension and also develop your vocabulary.

There are many words in the English language that sound similar but have totally different meanings. We looked at homophones in the spelling section in chapter 2, but these words are different. They have different spellings, and they mean something different, but they can be easily confused.

Some examples of this are *accept*, "to take something," and *except*, "to leave out," and *confident*, "to be sure of oneself," and *confidant*, "someone to confer with or tell a secret to."

Say the following commonly confused words aloud. You must listen carefully to ensure that you do not interpret the wrong meaning. As an alternative task, you can ask another person to read the two words to you and then write the meaning showing the difference between the words.

The first two are done for you as examples.

COMMONLY CONFUSED WORDS	MEANING/DIFFERENCE
a part/apart	A PART: a division of a whole APART: separated from
adopt/adapt	ADOPT: accept ADAPT: adjust
bazaar/bizarre	
dual/duel	
eminent/imminent	
entitle/title	
exalt/exult	
flounder/founder	
marital/martial	
moral/morale	
precedent/president	
turbid/turgid	

PREPOSITION FUN!

Best for: auditory processing, grammar, spatial awareness

This exercise will help you build your spatial awareness and practice using more specific and precise vocabulary.

People with dyslexia can experience difficulties with prepositions. Prepositions are words that can describe location, place, or time, such as *at, for, in, off, on, over, below,* and *under,* and this can be challenging.

Examples include the following:

- behind the house

- on the counter

- under the table

- down the hill

- in the sink

- above the bookcase

- in front of the desk

INSTRUCTIONS: Write a complete sentence for each of the following prepositions. If you find this challenging and do not know which preposition to use, try to visualize parts of a sentence. For example, you can visualize a park that has a fountain and children's playground. Place yourself between the two or inside or beside one of the locations. You can also model this with objects on a table using different objects to represent the park, fountain, playground, and yourself. This tactic uses multisensory strategies—visual, tactile, kinesthetic, and auditory—which are highly recommended for people with dyslexia.

PREPOSITION	SENTENCE
across	
along	
at	
between	
down	
from	
off	
upon	
within	

TRANSCRIBE THE SONG

Best for: auditory perception, listening skills

This exercise will help you practice while listening to music you enjoy!

We hear and listen to songs all the time. We often focus on the tune. Sometimes when we look at the lyrics, we find they're different from what we thought. This is due to our auditory perception and discrimination. People with dyslexia may have more difficulty with auditory processing, and it's a good idea to practice it as much as possible.

This activity requires the use of a song with a catchy tune.

INSTRUCTIONS: Select a song you have not heard before and listen to it on YouTube. Try to transcribe the first verse. You may have to play it a few times. Afterward, look up the lyrics from lyrics.com or azlyrics.com and check how accurate you were. Then play the song with the lyrics so you can match the two.

_____

_____

_____

_____

_____

GOLDEN GLOBE SPEECH

Best for: identifying key pieces of information, developing competence in auditory processing

This exercise will help you develop your written and spoken communication skills.

Auditory processing includes reading written language aloud. Writing and reciting speeches and raising discussion points at meetings can help develop auditory skills.

INSTRUCTIONS: Select a movie (preferably one that you have seen recently). Imagine you are the director of this movie, and you have won a Golden Globe, rising to the top of all the other nominees. You anticipated that you might win, so you have prepared a speech. Google the movie's cast and crew and create a speech as if you were the director of that movie.

Consider the following in writing your speech:

* Gratitude

* Humor

* Acknowledgment

* The movie

* Your career

_____

_____

_____

_____

_____

_____

_____

Recording your speech and playing it back to yourself can also help you be more competent as you note the pace of your speech, the pauses you make, and the emphasis you give to certain words.

PLACE *B, D, P,* AND *T* IN THE WORD

Best for: spelling, reading fluently, phonological processing

This exercise will help you distinguish between letters with similar sounds that can be easily confused.

Some letters have very similar sounds, and it's easy for people with dyslexia to confuse them.

The most commonly confused letters are *b, d, p,* and *t.* Learning which letter or sound is right comes from seeing a word often. Some words with these letters don't usually pose a problem, particularly if you use them frequently. However, longer and less frequently used words can be problematic. For example, in the word *elephant,* you need to remember that there's a *p* and not an *f,* or you can try to remember that *ph* makes the *f* sound.

INSTRUCTIONS: Insert the letter *B, D, P,* or *T* in each blank to form the correct words.

WORD	CLUE
A L _ H A _ E _	all the letters
A _ A _ _ L E	flexible
_ R U M _ E _	a brass instrument

(continued)

WORD	CLUE
C L I _ _ O A R _	used to write on
C U _ _ O A R _	place for storing food
E X _ E N _ A _ L E	no longer necessary
_ I S _ O S A _ L E	can be thrown out
_ A _ E R _ A C K	softcover book
_ R E _ I C _ A _ L E	likely to happen
U N _ E R _ U R _ E _	not worried or concerned
U _ G R A _ E	to make an improvement
S U _ _ O E N A E _	legally made to attend a court
_ R E S C R I _ E _	dictated
_ E C O M _ O S A _ L E	can be broken down and reabsorbed
S H I _ _ U I L D E R	person who builds seaworthy vessels
_ U _ L I C I Z E	to tell everyone
_ E _ _ L E S	decorative stones
_ U I L _ U _	collection

Visual and Spatial Activities

PICTURE CHALLENGE

Best for: developing visual imagery, sequencing skills

This exercise will help you provide more detail in your written work. You will be able to use more descriptive words when writing or even talking to someone.

INSTRUCTIONS: Read a page or a chapter from a book, or if you have difficulty reading, ask someone to read to you or listen to an audiobook. Then scan through the text or listen to it again. Finally, follow the prompts below.

1. Close your eyes and form a picture in your mind of what you think the text was about.

2. Discuss or say aloud what you are visualizing.

3. Draw a picture of what you saw in your mind. You don't have to be an artist. Stick figures work just fine. Remember, this is your own creation and may only make sense to you.

4. Add a splash of color if you can.

5. If it's a longer chapter, you can make several drawings taken from the beginning, middle, and end of the chapter. This can help with the sequencing of the action in the chapter.

When you're finished, you should have a visual and sequential record of what the text was about. The visuals are triggers or prompts to help you remember and retell the story.

To make it more challenging, on a separate sheet of paper write a paragraph describing the characters. Draw the main characters. Try to show the main features described by the author (for example, long hair, serious stare, and long arms). You can exaggerate these features to make them stand out.

PLAN YOUR LIVING SPACE

Best for: visual observation, visual planning, organization

This exercise will help with planning and organization. These skills can transfer to other areas, at work and also at home. Though primarily a visual activity, it also incorporates elements of visual-spatial skills.

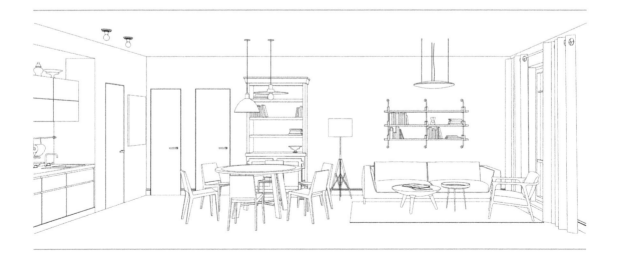

INSTRUCTIONS: Part 1. Draw pictures or icons to show how you would plan the layout of your house or apartment or a room within it and where the main furnishings would be placed.

INSTRUCTIONS: Part 2. For a more challenging exercise, design your home to scale. Show where the doors, rooms, and other elements would be and indicate the compass direction of the rooms (for example, south-facing).

PARADISE FOUND

Best for: visual tracking, processing speed

Mazes are a great way to build your directional skills. This exercise will also help with visual memory.

To prepare, you'll need a stopwatch to time yourself. It's a good idea to make photocopies of this activity to have on hand for whenever you want to practice your visual tracking skills with this exercise!

INSTRUCTIONS: With a pen, pencil, or other drawing tool, track the route to paradise. To vary the exercise and make it more challenging, work backward from the palm tree. Try this once a day and you should be able to do this faster each time!

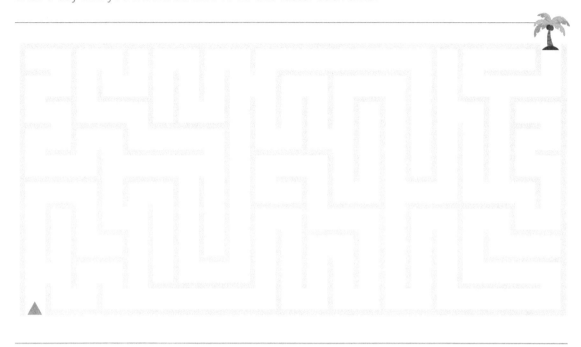

READ THE SIGNS

Best for: visual recognition, comprehension, environmental awareness

This exercise will help you translate the language of visual cues into meaningful written words.

One of the good points about visual communication is that it's universal. It does not rely on language and reading skills.

INSTRUCTIONS: Part 1. You're probably already familiar with these traffic signs. Look at each and write down what you think it means. Try to be a precise as possible.

——————— ——————— ——————— ———————

——————— ——————— ——————— ———————

INSTRUCTIONS: Part 2. After you complete the first exercise, try to make up some original signs for aspects of your workplace or for the environment.

DESCRIBE THE DIFFERENCES

Best for: visual perception, visual recognition, visual memory

This activity involves visual observation and how you might describe a visual image. Doing this helps you build visual awareness skills that can help with creative and descriptive writing.

Two photographs of birds are shown: the common kingfisher and the European goldfinch.

INSTRUCTIONS: Look at each photo for about 30 seconds. Then, without looking back at the photos, write down what you saw. Try to recall details like color, actions, contrast, and features in your descriptions.

For a more challenging exercise, describe the differences between the two photos.

INSPIRATIONAL IDEAS: SEEING THE UNSEEN

Best for: creative writing, creative thinking, using clues and inspiration from a photo

This activity will help you with creative writing and vocabulary.

In chapter 1, I mentioned the work of Tom West in relation to people with dyslexia being able to think outside the box. This activity aims to help you think outside the box and to draw inspiration from photos. The idea is for you to study the photos on this page and brainstorm some ideas sparked by the images. This could be anything from doing the weekly grocery shopping to penning a murder mystery novel! Everything, no matter what, starts through some inspirational idea, image, or even conversation. This activity is all about the use of images.

INSTRUCTIONS: Look at each photo. Then write about anything that comes to mind. It could be a description of the photo, a memory the image calls to mind, a dream you have, or something else.

_____

_____

_____

_____

_____

_____

PLAN YOUR NEIGHBORHOOD

Best for: developing visual-spatial skills, planning, organization, creativity

This exercise will help you with planning and with developing your awareness of the environment.

This activity is a follow-up to "Plan Your Living Space." For this one, you'll consider the different facilities in a neighborhood, such as houses, roads, sidewalks, parks, recreation centers, stores, library, and schools.

INSTRUCTIONS: Use the next page to plan a neighborhood. Draw elements such as homes, roads, bike lanes, bus lanes, parks, schools, community facilities, stores, medical facilities, street lighting, parks, galleries, and sports facilities.

As part of your planning, consider the questions in the following table. In the response column, explain your reasons for putting facilities where they are.

CONSIDERATION	RESPONSE
Are the schools in a safe location?	
Are the homes well spaced?	
Are there adequate community facilities?	
Are there sufficient transportation options?	
Are the stores conveniently located?	
Is there space for social interaction?	
Are there medical facilities?	
What about bike and bus lanes and street lighting?	

FIND GRAND CENTRAL TERMINAL, NEW YORK

Best for: map reading; sequencing information, directions

Putting the steps in the right sequence will help you build the skills necessary for following step-by-step directions (particularly those on your phone or a map) and finding your way from place to place.

INSTRUCTIONS: Put the directions in the following box in the proper order to get to Grand Central Terminal from Times Square. You are starting at Times Square.

Continue to Madison Avenue.

Head east to Bryant Park.

Head south to West 40th Street.

Take East 43rd Street to Grand Central Terminal.

Head east past 5th Avenue.

Go north across Bryant Park.

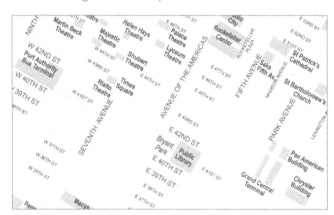

REMEMBER AND DRAW THE SHAPE

Best for: visual-spatial recognition, processing speed, memory

This exercise will help you build visual memory skills. These skills can transfer to many other areas and can help with visual awareness and general visual recognition and can also indirectly help with reading and spelling.

INSTRUCTIONS: Spend two minutes studying all the shapes, and then try to draw them without looking. (You can try this a second time while looking at the shapes.)

More challenging: Look at the shapes for one minute, and then draw all of them.

Most challenging: Look at all of the shapes for 30 seconds, and then draw all of them!

Once you complete the three timing options, challenge yourself by trying to beat your record time!

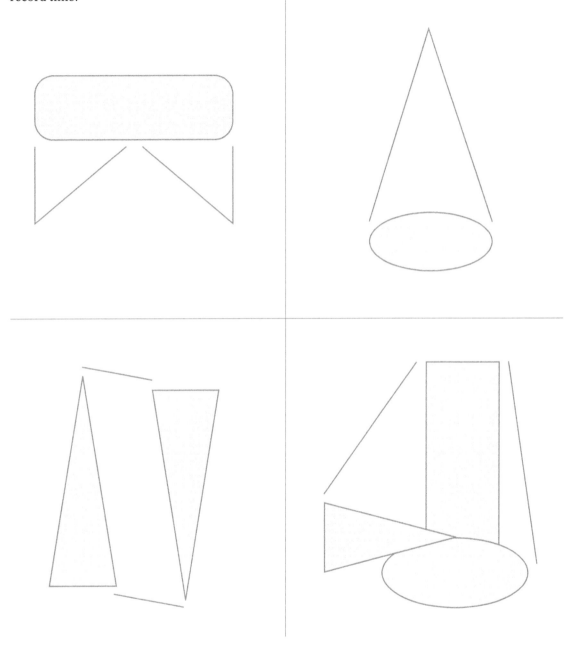

CHAPTER FOUR

MASTERING EXECUTIVE FUNCTIONING SKILLS

Try to imagine an orchestra with all the different instruments. Each member of the orchestra is skilled in using their own particular instrument, whether it be the cello, double bass, or violin. All the instruments are usually used together to make harmony. But the key player is the conductor, who coordinates the players and harmonizes and synchronizes the interactions among them. Without the conductor, the music would be hit or miss. The purpose of the executive functioning component of the brain is very much like that of the conductor of an orchestra.

Executive functions relate to controlling and organizing behavior. The planning, controlling, and monitoring of tasks and impulses are the primary roles of the executive functions. Executive functions also include working memory, attention, time management, flexible problem-solving, initiation, self-awareness, and impulse control.

For the adult with dyslexia, this can mean issues with the following:

- Attention (e.g., when being given instructions)

- Memory (losing or misplacing materials)

- Starting a task (knowing how to start and what to do first)

- Timekeeping (managing appointments and scheduling activities)

- Being easily overwhelmed (feeling the task is too big and being unable to break it down into manageable chunks)

- Forward planning and decision-making

- Controlling emotions

These factors can all be obstacles in the workplace and in life in general. It's important for you to be aware of these executive functions so you can prevent them from becoming too much of a barrier.

This chapter provides several activities on different aspects of executive functioning.

As with all the skills you're building, the more you practice, the more proficient and more successful you will become.

I do, however, want to reinforce the positive aspects of dyslexia. You can use your strengths as you're tackling the activities.

Executive Functioning Activities

SELF-KNOWLEDGE

Best for: recognizing the distractors, focusing and attention, staying on task

This activity will help you gain more control over your own learning. It will also help you develop more efficient learning strategies.

"We ought to begin to pay less attention to getting everyone over the same hill using the same path. We may wish to encourage some to take different routes to the same end. Then we might see good reasons for paying careful attention to their descriptions of what they have found. We may wish to follow them someday."

—Tom West, *In the Mind's Eye*

The very essence of this statement indicates that people with dyslexia have much to offer. They can lead rather than be led, be innovative and inventive, and can think outside the box. But it also means they need to know themselves—how they learn and their individual learning preferences. This knowledge can help learning become more effective, and it can help you harness maximum attention to the task at hand.

INSTRUCTIONS: Part 1. Answer the following self-discovery questions.

What factors/situations do you find the most distracting?

_____

_____

Why do you think these factors/situations are distracting?

_____

_____

How can you avoid them?

_____

_____

Make a list of some things that might help you concentrate better when learning and why you think these would help.

_____

_____

Are the things you identified the same for every type of learning, or do they depend on what type of activity you are doing?

_____

_____

INSTRUCTIONS: Part 2. Think about the different tasks you do and make a learning plan using the following table. You can use the first item as an example.

LEARNING PLAN

ACTIVITY	TIP TO IMPROVE CONCENTRATION	TIP TO ELIMINATE DISTRACTIONS
Reading	Make sure table light is not too bright. Read before 8 p.m. Set a timer to take breaks every hour.	Sit in a quiet place. Put cell phone in silent mode.

MNEMONICS

This exercise teaches you a memory strategy you can use in your everyday life.

A mnemonic is a memory strategy. It can be a phrase, picture, poem, image, acronym, or rhyme that can act as a trigger to recall information. This is particularly useful for tricky information like a difficult spelling or a list of items.

There are a number of different ways of constructing a mnemonic, but it is best if you construct the actual mnemonic from your own imagination. Sometimes the more ridiculous the mnemonic is, the easier it is to remember. Mnemonics can also be constructed using items in a room, such as a table, chair, wall, window, floor, door, desk, drawer, cupboard, or backpack.

Let's use the example of a commonly misspelled word to illustrate how mnemonics work. The word *separate* is often misspelled by people with dyslexia; they often use *ete* at the end instead of *ate*. The mnemonic could be: "There is a *rat* in *separate*."

INSTRUCTIONS: Try to make up some mnemonics for words you find tricky and for lists of things you need to remember. Use the strategies you like best, such as drawing pictures, taking photos, writing, or making audio recordings. Another example follows.

Tricky word: rhythm

Mnemonic: Rhythm helps your two lips move (creating an acronym for rhythm)

CHUNKING FOR SUCCESS

This exercise teaches you a convenient memory strategy for organizing and recalling information that has multiple components.

Chunking is a very successful strategy and one that I use all the time. The more you practice it, the easier it becomes. It involves grouping similar items together, and you get to decide what you mean by "similar." For example, for a grocery list, you may put all the cleaning items together and remember the number and/or the initials of each. Then you may put all the dairy products together, then the fruits, and then the vegetables.

You can use chunking for anything, including information you may need to recall for your social life or for presenting information to management or colleagues. An example most of us use without thinking is phone numbers. We put the area code into the first chunk and then divide the rest of the numbers into two other chunks.

Here are three tips for chunking:

1. Look for associations among the items to be remembered. For example, if you are going grocery shopping, you may want to remember all the bakery products you need in one chunk—this can be associated with the word *bakery* or a visual image of a baker's hat or a bagel. The idea is that you use whatever is most familiar to you. This will help you remember a group of items in the chunk.

2. Think of how you might remember the individual items in the chunk. For example, if you have three bakery items to remember, you may put them in alphabetical order and just remember the first couple of letters for each item. For example, if you are remembering bread, bagels, and butter (all items that begin with the letter b), you can use the first two letters so you remember *ba*, *br*, and *bu*. If these are the only items you need to remember, you could use just one letter for each: *a*, *r*, and *u* for *bagel*, *bread*, and *butter*.

3. Use visual imagery by picturing in your mind where an item belongs.

INSTRUCTIONS: Look at the following list of 22 items. Work out how you might use chunking to organize and remember the things on the list. What strategies can you use?

6 apples, 1 chicken, 1 box of table salt, 3 cans of tuna, dishwashing liquid, 6 red peppers, grapes, fabric softener, napkins, 2 melons, 1 bunch of bananas, 8 plums, 1 jar of raspberry jam, 1 package of frozen strawberries, 2 bars of soap, 3 peaches, cinnamon, 3 frozen pizzas, 1 container of oatmeal, 1 dozen free-range eggs, 2 gallons of milk, 3 tubes of toothpaste

_____

_____

_____

_____

_____

_____

PRACTICE MAKING CONNECTIONS

Best for: memory, comprehension

This exercise gives you practice making connections between things so you can understand, remember, and relay information to others.

Understanding can be the key to memory, particularly if you impose your own interpretation onto the item or idea that has to be remembered. Making connections between words, ideas, pieces of information, or concepts is important to understanding them.

Making connections helps with organization and can be very useful if you have to summarize information you're reading. You can make a connection to something in the world or to something you imagine as long as you understand the connection.

INSTRUCTIONS: Try this activity that consists of random words. Your goal is to connect at least two or more items together. The first few are done for you as examples.

WORD	CONNECTION	WHY?
bus	car	transportation
melons	cantaloupe	type of melon
movie	theater	where movies are shown

(continued)

WORD	CONNECTION	WHY?
cappuccino		
computer		
detergent		
economy		
music		
restaurant		

PRACTICE VISUALIZATION

Best for: developing memory skills and creativity and remembering sequencing

This exercise will help you build your visualization skills.

Visualization is a powerful tool to help with memory and retention of information. Sometimes this can come quite naturally, but some people need to practice visualization.

A good way to start is with mind mapping. Mind mapping is a very popular and established strategy, and you can refer to the Internet for examples.

INSTRUCTIONS: Begin with something familiar to create your own mind map, such as what you did over the weekend. You can divide your weekend into various activities and think of a visual image for each. For example, if you watched a football game, think of an image for the game. It may be the football, the teams lining up, the scoreboard, or something else. Try to visualize one image for each activity you did.

You'll need a central image and subdivisions for your weekend activities. These subdivisions could be family, sports, finance, television, and entertainment.

For a greater challenge, try to create a mind map of information you need for work or for a new activity you're learning. Any image will suffice. Using color in your visualization also helps you organize and remember.

BE ACTIVE, NOT PASSIVE

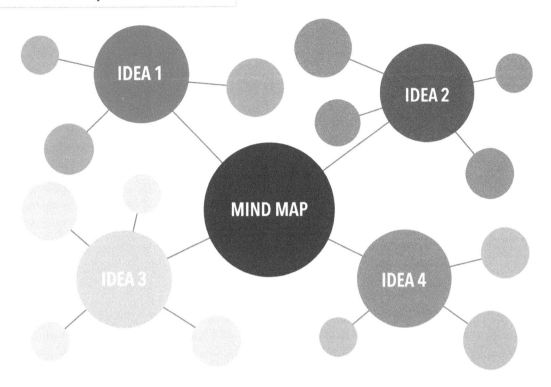

Best for: developing effective learning skills, revising information previously learned

This exercise will help you become an active learner.

There is a great deal of consensus that learning information actively is more effective than passive learning. This is particularly the case for adults with dyslexia. Reading in itself is quite passive, but if you discuss what you have read with another person, it becomes active! This is how information is retained and understood more clearly.

Examples of active learning include:

- Recording the information in written or audio form

- Discussing it with friends

- Inquiring further to gain more insights into the event/information

- Making some illustrations (perhaps a mind map) of the information

Why Do We Play Sports?

The first recorded Olympic Games were held in Athens in 776 BCE. It was more a celebration to honor the gods than a competition. The events included running, long jump, shot put, javelin, boxing, pankration (a mix of wresting and boxing), and equestrian sports. It soon, however, became very competitive. The Greeks enjoyed competition, and the games offered a great opportunity for athletic skills.

The games were also used like a calendar. The four-year interval between the ancient Olympic Games was named an "Olympiad" and was used for dating purposes at the time: time was counted in Olympiads rather than in years. The games continued to be celebrated when Greece came under Roman rule.

The modern-day Olympic ring symbol was designed by Baron Pierre de Coubertin in 1912. The idea of using rings intertwined with one another came from the Union des Sociétés Françaises de Sports Athlétiques (USFSA), which had two interlaced rings as its symbol.

The Olympic flag has a white background with five interlaced rings in the center: blue, yellow, black, green, and red. This design is symbolic: It represents the five continents of the world, united by Olympism, while the six colors are those that appear on all the national flags of the world at the present time.

Today the Olympics are both symbolic and prestigious. The event brings countries together, and an Olympic gold medalist becomes an iconic figure. Participating in the Olympic Games is the result of years of daily grind and strenuous training. This may beg the question "Why do we as individuals and as a country like sports?"

WRITE, RECITE, REPEAT, REVIEW, REINFORCE

Best for: organization, long-term memory, comprehension

This exercise will help you build the skills necessary for creating systems for remembering things.

One of the best memory strategies is to have a consistent system that you can use. In this activity, you will be using a "write, recite, repeat, review, and reinforce" method.

1. Write it down, as the actual process of writing can help strengthen the kinesthetic memory.

2. Recite it to yourself or others, as this strengthens the memory through both the speech and auditory channels.

3. Repeat it a number of times, as this can help you absorb information through the auditory channel.

4. Review the information to ensure you have fully understood it.

5. Reinforce it. This is the consolidation part, and it ensures that it is firmly in your long-term memory. To achieve this, you can ask yourself questions about the information, which helps with understanding and long-term retention. You can also use a mind map if you want to introduce visuals to help with retention.

This method is multisensory, which is considered the most effective way for adults with dyslexia to learn. It involves visual, auditory, kinesthetic, oral, and action (doing) learning.

INSTRUCTIONS: Try using the "write, recite, repeat, review, and reinforce" method with a piece of information/text you need to remember or know for your job.

For example, if you're a database programmer, you would need to know the names, sizes, and features of the latest software programs. If there is a privacy code for these, you would need to remember that, as well as any passwords. You would also need to know the troubleshooting formulas and solutions to common problems that might occur, as well as the names of customers and contacts.

TIPS

- Write some key points on small cards and carry these around with you.

- Try to use the repetition part as much as possible—while walking or during a break.

- Experiment by recording yourself while reciting and listen to the recording when you have the opportunity.

- Use visuals as much as possible.

SALON TIME

Best for: time management, organization, memory

This imaginative exercise will help you practice organizational as well as planning skills.

Whether running a business or living daily life, everyone is responsible for scheduling and some form of financial management.

INSTRUCTIONS: You are doing two days of scheduling for a friend who is a hairstylist. The client list and price list follow.

Create the schedule for two days and include how much income the hairstylist will receive. The hair stylist works from 9 a.m. to 5 p.m. each day, and she takes a 30-minute break in the morning and one hour for lunch at any convenient time in the afternoon.

CLIENTS ON DAY 1

Janette Jones: partial highlights and cut

Jake Forbes: cut and blow dry

Shelley Moore: cut

Mamoun Mohammed (age 12): cut

Yanik Bader: cut and color

CLIENTS ON DAY 2

Bill Caruthers: cut and blow dry

Lindsay Johnson: cut, partial highlights

Galia Rasheed: cut, full highlights

Joanne Selik: cut and blow dry/style

HAIRSTYLIST PRICE LIST

Cut: $50, 1 hour

Children's cut: $35, 30 minutes

Cut and blow dry/style: $65, 1.5 hours

Partial highlights: $90, 2 hours

Full highlights: $110, 2.5 hours

Cut and color: $85, 1.5 hours

DAY 1	DAY 2

PROBLEM-SOLVING

Best for: developing executive functioning, controlling impulses, planning

This activity will help you develop your monitoring and review skills.

Often when we have a task to complete, we go headfirst into it, perhaps without giving it sufficient forethought. This is a natural human approach. One of the jobs of the executive functioning part of the brain is to control impulses and to monitor and review how we are progressing with a task.

It's important to be aware of how we're thinking when we tackle a task and what we can learn from completing it.

INSTRUCTIONS: Part 1. Read the following story.

Dawn observed the rolling peaks with apprehension and excitement. Behind this adventure, she realized that hidden dangers lurked! To start, she had left a mess back at the cabin, and Ahmed was sure to stumble on a secret Dawn had been hiding from him for months now. She wished she had given some thought to this before her rather impetuous trek to the mountains. She was experienced in the mountains and well equipped, but there was more on her mind than ascending the triple peaks in the horizon.

Meanwhile, Ahmed had finally reached the deserted cabin and wasted no time in using this opportunity to unravel some suspicions he had harbored for months now. He did not want to believe Dawn was deceitful, but recent events had raised suspicion. He intended to get to the bottom of this!

INSTRUCTIONS: Part 2. Consider these three key concepts, and answer the questions:

1. THINK: What is Ahmed thinking, and what is he thinking of doing?

2. JUSTIFY: What do you think might justify these thoughts? Why might he have these thoughts?

3. ACTION: What action might Dawn take? Think of several different courses of action that can be taken. What advice can you give on how to proceed?

_____

_____

_____

_____

GO FOR GOAL

Best for: goal setting, obtaining targets, planning, motivation, time-management goals

This is a great activity for building the necessary skills for advance planning!

Planning for a goal or aim is very much an executive functioning role. Going for a goal is a journey, and for any journey, you need to know the route in advance. Often people with dyslexia have a concept of the goal but difficulty planning the route.

In this activity, you'll think about four possible goals. They can be hypothetical, and it may even be best if they are. You'll look at the strengths you can bring to achieving each goal and the obstacles that need to be overcome.

INSTRUCTIONS: Set your goals. A good one to start with is planning for a summer vacation. Now think of the obstacles you need to deal with to achieve the goal and how you'll deal with them.

GOAL	OBSTACLES	HOW TO DEAL WITH THE OBSTACLES

- Set a goal that's as specific as possible.

- Be clear about why you want to achieve this goal.

- Give yourself a time frame to achieve the goal.

- Reward yourself at each step and make it a big reward at the end.

BEGIN AT THE BEGINNING

Best for: getting started with a task, planning, self-monitoring

This strategy-building activity will help you overcome the roadblock of "getting started."

One of the most common statements adults with dyslexia make is "I am not sure how to begin this task." There are some genuine reasons for having difficulty in starting a task. You'll find some in the following table.

To overcome these obstacles, you first need to work out how to tackle them. Then you can approach them with confidence!

INSTRUCTIONS: Look at the following table. Add your own tactics to the general suggestions. Also add other obstacles you often experience and think how you might use tactics to overcome them.

OBSTACLE	TACTIC
Fear of failure	Break the tasks into chunks and look at each chunk separately.
Being overwhelmed	Break the tasks into chunks, but also work out a manageable time schedule for each task.

Something taking too long	A schedule will help here, and at this stage, determine how much time you want to allocate for the task. Setting a timer to go off periodically as a reminder to check on your time and progress may help.
Feeling others can do better than you	You are not competing with anyone. Set your own targets. Your progress is about you, not anyone else.

TIME TO ORDER

Best for: organization, memory, accessing information, planning

This activity will help you build organizational skills for better learning and memory.

Any type of information will be recalled more effectively if it's organized. This is the key to a good memory. You may be more concerned with finding the information you need than organizing it and putting it into categories. But information can be remembered more effectively if it's organized at the point of learning. Organization also helps with understanding and retention.

Following is the information processing cycle. Each of the three stages is essential.

- **Input**
  - » Taking information in through reading, listening, or watching

- **Processing**
  - » Learning the information
  - » Absorbing the new information
  - » Incorporating it into your existing understanding

- **Output**
  - » Reporting on the information
  - » Preparing the information for written or oral presentation

Example:

- **Input.** Take notes during the sales call with your potential client about the problems they are currently facing and how they have already tried to solve them. Ask pertinent questions to illicit responses that will give you a framework of their current needs, obstacles, and budget.

- **Processing.** Review your notes from the call, asking yourself how you can help the client solve their current problem, how your company will be a better option than the competition, and what additional value you can offer them to sweeten the deal.

- **Output.** Organize your ideas and prepare a detailed, one-page sales presentation outlining the products you think will be best suited to your potential client to help them solve their problem and achieve their goals. You may also want to think of a catchy phrase to sum up your idea.

You can apply the "input, processing, output" strategy to any task in your personal or professional life that would benefit from an ordered approach.

INSTRUCTIONS: Locate some information, such as a magazine article, a work-related document, or something else that interests you. Practice how you might organize that information using the information processing cycle strategy to help you retain it for future reference.

READY TO ORDER

Best for: executive functioning, organization, setting priorities

This exercise will help you analyze a big task and turn it into a more manageable one.

It's Friday afternoon, and you've had a hectic week. You look at your desk or workspace and are confronted with a pile of paper and notes. You also have sticky notes plastered on the wall. You want to clear this mess or at least organize it so you can start with a clean slate on Monday. You may not clear all the tasks, but at least you'll know how to get started on Monday!

INSTRUCTIONS: Look at the seven tips that follow and write out how you might spend the last hour of Friday afternoon preparing for Monday. You'll find it helpful to relate this to your own work or to something at home you could approach better with a system in hand. Remember to reflect when finished. This is very important, as it helps with self-awareness and an understanding of your own learning style.

ORGANIZE AND SUCCEED: SEVEN TIPS

1. Outline the task before you start.

2. Break the task down into smaller pieces.

3. Set dates for working on smaller tasks (mini goals).

4. Make a priority list.

5. Make your own schedule of how to use your time.

6. Self-monitor by identifying what you need to deal with now and what you can leave until later.

7. Reflect when finished. What did you do well? How can you learn from this?

_____

_____

_____

_____

_____

MANAGING TIME: THE PPRR STRATEGY

Best for: time management, organization, working more efficiently

This exercise will help you manage your time and feel less overwhelmed by the tasks ahead!

Oh, that Monday-morning feeling! We can get overwhelmed at times when we look at all the tasks we need to do for the coming week—both at work and at home. This can range from writing reports to paying bills to leading meetings. Sometimes just responding to emails can take up a massive chunk of time.

To help, try the "PPRR" strategy: prioritize, plan, respond, reflect.

INSTRUCTIONS: Jot down some major tasks you have to complete in the next day, week, or month. Then fill out the table by following this formula:

- **Prioritize.** Once you have noted all the tasks you have to complete, code them from 1 to 4: 1 = urgent, 2 = important, 3 = can be left until later, and 4 = do I really need to do this?

- **Plan.** Now look at the tasks and the codes you have assigned to them, decide when you will tackle the urgent tasks, and insert them into your schedule. Then insert the others in order of priority. Try to be as precise as possible, but leave some extra time for the unexpected.

- **Respond.** Now you are ready to tackle the first task. You will have allocated time, so no need to panic or hurry. Your total focus should be on this task only! Remember to break down the task into manageable units.

- **Reflect.** This is an important part of time management. Reflection involves going through what you have done and asking yourself:

  » Did I reach my targets?

  » Did I use my time efficiently?

  » What factors distracted me or prevented me from using my time efficiently?

  » How can I improve my time-management skills?

PRIORITIZE	PLAN	RESPOND	REFLECT
In order of urgency	When will I do these?	Do I need to do anything else; for example, contact people or read reports?	Did I accomplish this? Did I learn any new ideas or strategies? Are there any areas for improvement?
1.			
2.			
3.			
4.			

MAKE UP YOUR MIND!

Best for: decision-making, executive functions, evaluation, critical thinking

This exercise will help you develop the important self-talk skills necessary for thinking through decisions.

Decision-making is an important part of executive functioning that relates to what is called *inhibitory control*. This is the ability to control impulses, keep distractions in check, and pause and think before acting out or making a decision.

Self-monitoring and self-talk are forms of inhibitory control. Self-monitoring is important for impulse control and subsequent decision-making. Self-talk is an effective way to keep thoughts and potential actions uppermost in your mind. When occasions arise that provoke strong negative emotions or feelings of failure, self-talk can help identify potential problematic thinking and behavior patterns.

Self-talk can take the form of imagining that a significant person who has given you good advice in the past is speaking to you now.

You can see that after considering various outcomes, you come to a final decision. This process is very much part of executive functioning. Consider a new house purchase, for example. The problem is whether to buy. You can do nothing and not buy. If you buy, you will have less money to spend, or you could buy a cheaper house in a better location.

You then make a decision to make an offer on the house, and the outcome of that is you may have to take a second job, but you would enjoy the amenities of the new home. You buy the house, find it is affordable, and just eat out less than before.

INSTRUCTIONS: Think of a dilemma or decision you have to deal with. It can be work-related or personal. Write down the factors you might consider. For example, if you were thinking of putting an offer on a new house, you may say, "Is it the right location? Why is the location good or not so good? Is the accommodation better than what I have at the moment? Can I afford it? If I bought it, what might I have to go without?" You can do this by using what is known as a "decision tree," pictured here for someone deciding whether to rent or buy.

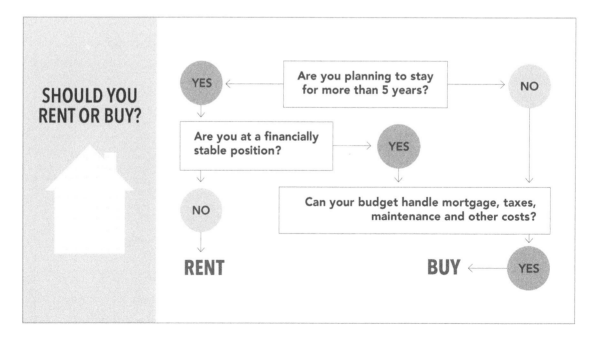

BE PREPARED

Best for: anticipating questions, preplanning, interviews, listening skills

This activity will assist you in preparing for interviews and explore questions you may like to ask yourself when considering an opportunity.

Anyone can become flustered when faced with questions in tricky situations, such as interviews. These situations can be particularly challenging for people with dyslexia. Quite often after an interview, people with dyslexia say, "Why didn't I think of that before?"

It's a good idea to try to anticipate questions you may be asked. This can apply to interviews, customers on the phone, your boss, your work colleagues, or an exam you're planning to take for some additional qualification.

For example, here are some questions you may ask yourself prior to an interview:

- Why do I want this job?

- What do I know already about the job?

- What more do I want to know?

- What is the long-term future of the company and my role?

- What additional training might I need?

- How am I equipped to do this job?

- Why should this company employ me?

- In what way is my previous experience helpful for this job?

INSTRUCTIONS: Imagine your manager has offered you a different job or role. Note some questions you might ask yourself before accepting it and write your response to them.

_____

_____

_____

_____

USING EXECUTIVE FUNCTIONING SKILLS TO HELP WITH STUDYING

Best for: preparing for studying, exams, effective learning

This exercise will help you find the ideal study formula for yourself. To do that, it's worth the time to first do some self-discovery.

One of the most effective strategies for learning something new is to know yourself. What kind of learner are you? Once you know, you can prepare to educate yourself with a process and tools that will bring out your best qualities.

INSTRUCTIONS: Part 1. Dig into discovering the type of learner you are! The following table explains different learning styles.

LEARNING STYLE	WHAT YOU WOULD GAIN
Auditory	You will be able to find out information and are likely to do this by making lists and perhaps discussing the new information with someone.
Visual	You will gain most from your learning by using drawings and diagrams to understand and retain information. You will also benefit from using videos and computer programs.
Kinesthetic	You will gain most from visits and activities and from experiencing new things.
Persistent	You will be able to persist with lengthy tasks, and this learning style can help with problem-solving activities.
Global	You will gain most by looking at the big picture and obtaining an overview of the information. You will also benefit from short tasks with frequent breaks and lots of discussion.

LEARNING STYLE	WHAT YOU WOULD GAIN
Social	You need other people to help you sound out ideas. You can also help them as you can come up with suggestions for them, too. It is best for you to work in groups or in pairs and have lots of discussion.
Metacognitive	You are good at problem-solving and thinking about the pros and cons of a dilemma. You are self-aware and know the best way for you to tackle a problem.
Tactile	You need to make something! You will prefer hands-on learning. Making models and planning and undertaking demonstrations would be good for you.

INSTRUCTIONS: Part 2. Now put it all together! Fill out the following table to be prepared the next time you study. Refer to the preceding learning style table as needed. A sample response is provided.

WHAT DO I WANT TO LEARN?	HOW WILL I DO THIS?	WHERE AM I GOING TO GET THE INFORMATION?	WAS I SUCCESSFUL? IF NOT, WHY? WHAT ELSE CAN I DO?
more about climate change	I am very visual, so I will watch videos.	Internet, YouTube	I learned a lot but need more critical opinions. I will need to watch some interviews with world leaders and well-known activists.

MOTIVATE FOR SUCCESS

Best for: developing self-awareness and self-esteem

This exercise will help you reflect on what specifically motivates you and how you can work toward it.

Motivation is one of the key areas of learning. Although there are different elements that trigger motivation, it can be a component of executive functioning.

INSTRUCTIONS: Part 1: Spend some time reviewing the four kinds of motivation.

MAIN TYPES OF MOTIVATION

- **Motivation by Task**

  » An achievable task that is broken down into small steps

- **Social Motivation**

  » The influence of peer groups

- **Motivation by Feedback**

  » Continuous feedback that fosters growth and development

- **Motivation by Achievement**

  » How much the goal is desired or needed by the learner

INSTRUCTIONS: Part 2. Think of a task you have to do and answer the following questions to discover your own motivation formula.

MOTIVATION BY TASK

Have I read the instructions?

Do I know how to start the task?

Are there going to be challenging elements I can deal with before starting?

Do I know how long the task might take?

Can I arrange the timing so I am not rushed?

What will I gain from doing the task?

What will I now be able to do after completing the task?

MOTIVATION BY FEEDBACK

Am I expecting feedback, and do I know when I will get it?

What kind of feedback would be helpful?

Will the feedback tell me what I can do to improve?

Can I respond to the feedback?

CHAPTER FIVE

COPING STRATEGIES FOR THE STRESSORS OF DYSLEXIA

It's generally accepted that positive self-esteem is crucial for effective and successful learning. This applies to those with dyslexia and especially to dyslexic adults. Usually they have experienced many years of frustration and failure and feelings of inadequacies at school and sometimes beyond school. Although the initial issue may relate to academic work, including reading and writing, the challenges soon impact other areas that may not be concerned with school at all. In adulthood, people may find that the ongoing issues related to their dyslexia affect them socially and personally, in their family life and relationships with others. But it's certainly not all doom and gloom. Resilience is the key, and many people with dyslexia have outstanding resilience, determination, and abilities!

Coping with life's stressors is essential for anyone, including adults with dyslexia. Stress is not due to one single thing but is usually caused by a number of potential stressors working at the same time. If you're experiencing a number of stressors, then your resilience to stress will be lower. This means that perhaps one more stressful situation can send you over the edge! The saying "the straw that broke the camel's back" is so true with regard to stress. The last straw that sends someone into an extremely stressful state can be something like not being able to locate the correct phone number or missing the bus for work. These individual events would not usually send someone into a high state of stress, but if other things in their life are not going well, then something small can easily act as a catalyst for over-the-top stress.

Personal Life Stressors

Most people have to deal with a range of personal life stressors. People with dyslexia usually have additional stressors as well. These additional stressors can include communication issues, perhaps with a spouse or with friends; frustration at having difficulty with tasks that many find easy; low self-esteem that can result in stress from feeling inadequate; scheduling problems when having to make personal and family appointments and remembering these appointments, even though they may be on their calendar; and decision-making.

In conversations with friends, they may find they forget the end of a story or the name of a movie even though they know the information well. This kind of "it was on the tip of my tongue" phenomenon is characteristic of dyslexia and can cause frustration leading to stress. The accumulation of minor stressful situations that might seem not too important to others can feel overwhelming to the person who experiences them. It's important, therefore, to ensure that adequate supports are available and that your emotional concerns are taken seriously.

Workplace Stressors

Clearly, some workplace tasks will have a negative impact on the person with dyslexia, particularly if no accommodations for dyslexia are made.

Some of the potential workplace stresses include:

* Being given too many instructions at the same time

* Following a work manual that's not adequately adapted for someone with dyslexia

* Being required to read reports and present the findings quickly

* Reading lengthy emails and responding to them in writing

* Having to immediately recall telephone numbers

* Taking notes at meetings

* Performing administrative duties like filing documents and scheduling

* Having to multitask under pressure, such as writing messages while speaking on the phone or watching a screen

These factors, even one or two of them, can result in frustration, anger, and perhaps embarrassment if experienced by the person with dyslexia. Certainly, the person with dyslexia can try to build their own coping mechanism and develop resilience to help them deal with this. But employers can help by ensuring that the work environment is potentially stress-free and that accommodations for dyslexia are in place.

Creating and finding an accommodating workplace is difficult because of the nature of dyslexia. It has been described as a hidden disability for good reason. Many employers do not have a good understanding of dyslexia. And where there's a competitive job market, the dyslexic person may not be able to display and access their full potential in existing circumstances and environments. There needs to be a wider and more accurate understanding of the attributes of people with dyslexia and their potential.

Activities

The activities in this chapter are essentially of two types: *direct action* and *palliative* exercises. Direct action is often seen as a strategy for dealing with stress. This means you try to identify the problem and work out a way of either minimizing it or eradicating it altogether. For example, if the stressor is work overload, then simple direct action would lessen the load! This may be more difficult than it sounds, but the steps to doing this would also be classified as direct action.

The other means of dealing with stress is by using a palliative approach. Such approaches do not tackle the actual problem but attempt to equip the mind and body to cope with the stressors more easily. Yoga is a good example of a palliative approach to stress, as it attempts to relax the body and clear the mind. The intended result is for the person to feel refreshed and more relaxed and, therefore, more able to deal with their challenging issues and stressors. Sleep can also be palliative. It is nature's way of refreshing the body and mind.

KNOW YOUR EMOTIONS: SELF-KNOWLEDGE

Best for: knowing how to prevent stress, dealing with stress

This activity can help to defuse feelings of frustration by making you aware of what is causing them. Understanding is the first step toward doing something positive about the stressful situation.

Self-knowledge is a key factor in preventing stress. By knowing yourself and how you react to certain situations, you can either try to avoid those situations or prepare for them in advance. To achieve self-knowledge, you need to ask questions of yourself. It's not your perception of yourself you're looking to confirm by asking these questions; instead, you're learning how you react to and deal with certain situations.

Four factors are integrated into self-knowledge and stress: anger, fear, sadness, and happiness.

INSTRUCTIONS: Examine each self-knowledge factor using the following checklist. The first one is done for you as an example. There are also blank spaces for you to insert some other situations you have experienced. Once complete, look at each scenario and ask yourself why you feel that way. Identifying why you react as you do is the first step to being able to do something positive about it!

SITUATION	ANGER	FEAR	SADNESS	HAPPINESS
disagreement with a friend	✓		✓	
too much work				
commuting to work				
family squabbles				
feeling inadequate				
unhappy at work/not working				
your dyslexia				
missed opportunities				
weekend get-togethers				

MAKE A NOTE: MY STRESS CHART

Best for: identifying areas of stress, dealing with stress, avoiding stress

This activity will help you identify your stressors and monitor how you are dealing with them.

Keeping a stress chart can be useful for managing stress. To begin, note all the activities you do in one week, with the goal of building up to an entire month.

INSTRUCTIONS: For each stressful event, note:

- the time and day

- the stressful event

- the stress level on a 10-point scale

- the reason it was stressful

- how you reacted

The idea behind this activity is to help you put your stressors in perspective by identifying which activities are the most stressful and why you might want to avoid them. It can also help you identify how you can better deal with those that are unavoidable so they don't create so much stress.

DAY AND TIME	I BECAME STRESSED WHEN . . .	LEVEL OF STRESS	REASON I WAS STRESSED AND HOW I REACTED
Monday			
Tuesday			
Wednesday			
Thursday			

(continued)

DAY AND TIME	I BECAME STRESSED WHEN . . .	LEVEL OF STRESS	REASON I WAS STRESSED AND HOW I REACTED
Friday			
Saturday			
Sunday			

EAT, DRINK, WALK, AND SLEEP

Best for: healthy body and healthy mind, preventing stress

This activity will help you reflect on your lifestyle and make any changes toward a healthier and happier lifestyle.

There's a great deal of evidence that a healthy body can lead to a healthy mind and vice versa. Stress is therefore a whole-body phenomenon and not only a mental one. Yet in today's society, we tend to separate the two.

Hippocrates, the Greek physician who is often referred to as the father of modern medicine, said, "Walking is the best medicine."

The important factor is to create a balance. Too much exercise or indeed too much of anything may not be totally wise. You need to find your own personal balance.

Eating fresh and healthy foods, drinking plenty of water, walking regularly every day, and sleeping well and sufficiently give you the solid foundation for coping with potential stressors.

INSTRUCTIONS: Use the following table to chart your daily habits for the next week. Noting your habits can be useful for recognizing what you could use more of (like sleep!), and these may relate to the stress you experience. You can set yourself reasonable goals based on your completed table.

Daily Recommendations: (Note: These recommendations vary depending on your age and current health status.)

| 1-3 MILES | 5-9 SERVINGS | HALF BODY WEIGHT IN OUNCES | 7-9 HOURS |

DAY	WALKING	FRUIT AND VEGETABLES	WATER	SLEEP
Monday				
Tuesday				
Wednesday				
Thursday				
Friday				
Saturday				
Sunday				

CREATIVITY CAN KEEP YOU CALM

Best for: dealing with stressful periods and distractions from stress

This activity can help with inner reflection. The resulting calmness can help you put things into perspective.

Creativity is almost the same as escapism. Watching a movie that's totally absorbing can help you forget about any stressors you are experiencing in your life. When you are creative, you are also absorbed in and focused on an activity.

Creativity does not need to be Nobel Prize material. It can be anything you enjoy, such as solving a jigsaw puzzle, writing a poem, building your own kitchen cabinet, or landscaping your yard. Additionally, you'll also get a sense of accomplishment! Doing something creative can alleviate your stress and give you a sense of calm.

Creativity uses the right side of the brain. When engaged in a creative activity, you are apt to switch off the left side—which is more analytical and methodical—and be more intuitive and artistic and perhaps less preoccupied with what is around you.

INSTRUCTIONS: For this exercise, think of unusual and creative uses for the following and write down your ideas. Follow up by acting on some of them and enjoy your own way of being creative!

puddle of water

watering can

football

stepladder

picture frame

empty drink carton

_____

_____

rubber band

_____

_____

paper clip

_____

_____

flowerpot

_____

_____

tennis racket

_____

_____

Best for: displaying your creativity, random thinking

This follow-up activity can help you practice creativity in a safe environment. You won't be taking any risks, and it's good to practice and try to develop your creativity. You may find that you have skills that you were not aware of!

You may think that you are not very creative. But creativity can come in all shapes and sizes, for example, thinking of different uses for an empty tissue box, bottle tops, empty paper towel rolls, or empty coffee cups.

INSTRUCTIONS: Try to think of other uses for an everyday object you have in your home. Your ideas may not result in works of gallery art, but you are being creative and inventive. Sketch out one of your ideas here. You may even be inspired to make your invention!

COMMUNICATION IS COOL

Best for: discussing feelings, sharing worries and concerns

This exercise can help you articulate what is on your mind, and this can be a form of stress relief.

Stress is not always visible, as many people who are stressed often put on a brave public face. Hiding your stress in this way can be quite detrimental to your well-being and may hinder your ability to deal with it. While communicating with others about your personal or professional issues can be difficult, it can be the first step in alleviating stress and feelings of worry.

Consider the following pros and cons of communication.

PROS	CONS
It can be a relief to talk to someone.	You may feel vulnerable.
Another person might put the issues in perspective.	You may feel you are a burden to someone else.
Other people may have experienced similar issues and may have ways to deal with them.	It may not be helpful, and once you've spoken about an issue, you cannot take it back.
You might realize that you're not alone in feeling stressed.	If you speak to a work colleague or manager, it may have an adverse impact on your job.
Your stressors may seem more manageable than some other people's, and this may give you confidence to take action.	You may feel you are wasting someone else's time as you feel you should be able to handle your issue yourself.

Thinking about these pros and cons can lead you to knowing how best to communicate about your stressors and to whom. It's usually better to communicate than not to, but it may be difficult to find the words. Remember that communication is crucial to a healthy work environment. In 2017, the mantra for International Stress Awareness Day was "Speak Up and Speak Out About Stress." Face-to-face communication is often better than using technology to share your worries and stress.

FIVE TIPS FOR COMMUNICATION

1. **Prepare.** Know how you'll start and what you want to say.

2. **Relax.** Try to lighten the conversation to begin with, breathe slowly and relax, or go for a walk before the meeting.

3. **Don't expect an immediate response.** You're not looking for answers at this point, just sharing and caring. You can say that to put the other person at ease, too.

4. **Try to be straight and don't hide any information that can be helpful to the other person.** It's a good idea to give examples of what you mean.

5. **Be grateful.** Not everyone wants to listen to other people's problems, and it's good to have a listener even if they don't give you any answers.

One important point to emphasize is the need to prepare when sharing stressors with someone else. Sometimes the first sentence or phrase is important.

INSTRUCTIONS: Think of a stressful situation you have experienced or could experience. You may want to jot down some notes to describe the situation. Then think of some possible openers to a meeting with someone about your stress using the following table. The first one is an example. Try to do four others.

STRESS	OPENER
Heavy workload	I am sure you realize I am working weekends, too.

SHED AND SHRED

Best for: dealing positively with stress, taking the initiative

This activity can help you put things in order. You can see what is important and what is necessary and declutter your mind and your everyday work.

Sometimes a cluttered mind can blur your thinking and make it more difficult to put potentially stressful situations in perspective. Similarly, an overload of work duties and personal commitments can contribute to stress and also make it more difficult to get time to think and see things clearly. This activity is about offloading things that are causing you stress, whether it's clutter in the form of paper items you've held on to or activities and commitments that you don't have time for. You'll be shedding some duties, commitments, or tasks, and then shredding papers and information you've kept but do not need to keep. There is a saying "I can find anything for everything!" So, it might be useful to minimize everything.

INSTRUCTIONS: For this activity, you'll be thinking of weekly tasks you do and working out which column they go into. I've done a hypothetical one to get you started.

WHAT CAN I SHED?

TASK	REALLY IMPORTANT	WANT TO KEEP	MAY SHED
Baseball practice three times weekly			Can do twice weekly instead

DO THE SAME FOR ANY PAPERS YOU CAN SHRED.

WHAT CAN I SHRED?

PAPERS	REALLY IMPORTANT	WANT TO KEEP	MAY SHRED
Paper bank statements			Shred (first ensure that online statements are available)

LET IT BE

Best for: relaxation techniques to minimize stress

This activity can help you develop a more relaxed lifestyle. Regularly doing activities like this can also help with sleep and a sense of inner calmness.

A line from the popular Beatles song "Let It Be" says, "And when the night is cloudy, there is still a light that shines on me." That is a positive message, and it means that even when you think all is lost and you begin to despair, there will always be something that can help you become more positive. To do this you need to take the initiative and get yourself into a positive and relaxed frame of mind. There are lots of different ways of doing this and different types of relaxation exercises. Find one that is best suited to you. The message from an earlier activity in this chapter holds here, too: Eat, drink, walk, and sleep. You need to consider your whole body and your mind.

INSTRUCTIONS: Follow the steps in this progressive relaxation activity. You may like to have soft music on during this exercise.

1. Make sure you are lying comfortably and warm.

2. Become aware of your breath.

3. Start at your feet, tensing the muscles and then relaxing them.

4. Do this to other parts of your body, continuing to move up until you reach your face.

5. Do the same with all parts of you face and head.

6. Lie still for a few moments and try to clear your mind. At this point, you can also think of a relaxing image like a stream or beach.

7. You can stay there in peaceful thoughts for as long as you feel comfortable.

8. You may end with a mantra, such as "I am happy" or "I feel relaxed."

9. Sit quietly and spend a moment reflecting on how you feel.

BE POSITIVE

Best for: decision-making, creating successful opportunities

Some people have a tendency to automatically look for problems, and this leads them to develop a defeatist attitude at the outset. This exercise will help you see the good side of things!

It's quite easy for someone with dyslexia to feel overwhelmed and perhaps deflated when tackling some tasks. Being positive and ensuring you have healthy self-esteem are important and are accomplished through success. Success does not have to be monumental. It can be the satisfaction that comes from something small, like finishing a task in the time allocated or being happy with a purchase you've made.

Some people have to reassess what they understand success to mean. Remember that you are not measuring yourself against anyone else. Success is a personal attribute. You set the parameters, and you decide the outcome.

It's easy to confuse the idea of success with that of achievement. You can be successful without reaching any dizzy heights of achievement. Certainly, achievement can contribute to success. Success is a step-by-step process that builds on smaller achievements. Throughout the process, you can expect times of stagnation or little progress. It's not a straight line; rather, success is a process of curves, bends, and maybe even downward slides.

Let's illustrate with an example. You may want to walk more often to work. Imagine that the distance is walkable and would take you around 35 minutes. The reason you drive is because you often have papers and materials to take home, and you're always rushing in the morning.

You can set up some steps to achieve your goal.

The first thing you may want to do is to check exactly how long the walk will take you. Try to walk at a casual pace—no speed walking. You could then:

- Consider what you need to bring home with you. Try to restrict this as much as possible.

- Try to leave your workplace as punctually as possible so you're not tempted to take public transportation or a ride share as a time-saving action.

- Review your morning routine. This can include:

  » Setting your alarm clock slightly earlier

  » Preparing you work bag the night before

  » Packing your lunch the night before

- Try listening to music or an audiobook to help you enjoy the walk more.

  » Set reasonable targets for yourself—like walking to and from work twice weekly—and then build up to more.

  » Remember to always reward yourself every week, no matter how much or little you have achieved that week.

INSTRUCTIONS: Now take your own situation, whatever that might be, and work out what positive steps you can take to reach your goal.

Something I want to accomplish or do

_____

_____

Positive steps I can take

_____

_____

_____

_____

_____

CHAPTER SIX

STRENGTH-BUILDING STRATEGIES

This chapter will look at strength-building for people with dyslexia and focus on not what they cannot do but what they can do.

There's no doubt that people with dyslexia encounter real challenges—at school, in further education, and in the workplace. I cannot minimize the impact of these challenges as they are real and can have an enduring impact on the individual. At the same time, society's perception of dyslexia is beginning to change. People have begun to view dyslexia as a difference, not a disability, and many people with dyslexia have achieved great success. This is true of both famous personalities and those who are not in the public eye. They're doing a good job at work, are respected by colleagues, and are admired for their creativity and different ways of problem-solving. Many companies now see employees with dyslexia as a considerable asset to the company. These changes in perception, in addition to the findings of current research, have resulted in the words "dyslexia is a gift" being used more widely and believed more readily.

Studies of brain activity suggest that people with dyslexia have an underdeveloped left hemisphere language network. However, the right hemisphere compensates and can take over some of the tasks normally associated with the left hemisphere. And the right hemisphere of people with dyslexia tends to be strong in several areas, including visual processing, creativity, abstract thinking, and spatial ability, as well as comprehension activities.

There is now no need to hush up dyslexia. In fact, students applying for college or a job are encouraged to reveal that they have dyslexia. It's no longer seen as a stigma; it's no longer necessary to hide it! Race car driver Sir Jackie Stewart emphasized this when he talked openly about his own dyslexia and the importance of promoting dialogue that leads to better understanding.

Now the term *neurodiversity* is frequently used to describe the skills and potential of people with learning differences, including dyslexia. Neurodiversity takes the perspective that it's normal for people to have differences in the way their brains work. The neurodiversity movement is very positive and has gained a considerable impetus in recent years, which has helped change attitudes and misconceptions. This change, of course, starts in childhood—a point that has been prioritized by the neurodiversity movement.

This chapter features a range of activities to help you identify and develop your strengths as a person with dyslexia. These strengths include creativity, imagination, visual planning, facility with discussion, and visual-spatial skills. You may find some of the activities challenging, but the rewards make them worth tackling. As you practice and build your strengths, you'll become better at these tasks. It's my hope that these activities will give you confidence you can carry into all aspects of your life. Have fun!

Strength-Building Activities

WHY, OH, WHY?

Best for: creative thinking, investigation, thinking outside the box

This activity can increase your comprehension when people use phrases or words you don't know. This activity can also increase your own word power and confidence.

We use many common words, phrases, and idioms but rarely if ever give a thought to their origin. For example, the phrase *pros and cons* comes from an abbreviation of the Latin phrase *pro et contra*, which means "for and against." According to the *Oxford English Dictionary*, it's been in use in the abbreviated form since the 16th century!

People with dyslexia can have sudden insights into problem-solving and often use an unusual approach. They can think intuitively, letting their brain drift and come up with a solution. You can build this strength with the following activity.

INSTRUCTIONS: Guess the origins of the following words and phrases, and then look them up on the Internet to see if your definitions match what you learned. Use the table to fill in your responses, including drawings if you want to exercise even more or your creative skills.

WORD OR PHRASE	GUESS	INTERNET ANSWER
salary	something to do with sales	Egyptian empire laborers were paid in salt so they could preserve their food—this method was continued at the time of the Roman Empire, and it took the name salary.
berserk		
break the ice		
butterfingers		
chauffeur		
disaster		
Don't throw out the baby with the bathwater.		
quarantine		
quiz		

(continued)

WORD OR PHRASE	GUESS	INTERNET ANSWER
whiskey/whisky—why are there two spellings?		
your own idea: _____		

GRAPHIC ORGANIZER

Best for: visualization, organization, creativity

This activity will help you see and understand things at a glance. It can also give support in structuring new information visually to help with comprehension and organization.

People with dyslexia often prefer to think in pictures. They can become quite skilled at this, and everything they're involved in can become much clearer for them.

A graphic organizer provides a visual method of organizing any kind of information that needs to be understood, arranged, and recalled. A graphic organizer can be any form of visual design. It can be linear or random. It can be in the shape of a wheel or speech boxes. Its structure can be helpful in keeping you on track.

INSTRUCTIONS: Part 1. For a book or magazine article you've read or a movie you've seen, input the important information into a graphic organizer. Here is a template to get you started.

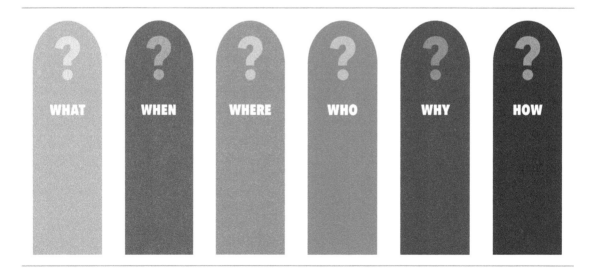

INSTRUCTIONS: Part 2. Now create your own graphic organizer for your leisure or work activities. The steps might include the following:

1. Decide what you want to organize.

2. Note all the associated activities. For example, if you're creating a graphic organizer for your leisure activities, write all the activities you'll be doing in the week.

3. Decide how you want to display them. Will you arrange them in a chart, circles, day-by-day planner, or activity themes, such as *sports*, *social*, and *relaxation*?

4. Place each activity into the organizer. You can write, draw, or even make an icon of the activity.

5. You can use color to give order to the importance of the activities.

6. Then you can take a photo of the organizer and keep it on your phone for reference.

INVENTION AND INNOVATION TIME

Best for: creativity, imaginative thinking, visual development

This is a fun activity that will help you be creative with no rules at all. There is no right or wrong answer—you decide and create!

People with dyslexia tend to be good at thinking outside the box. They can take an object and use it in a novel way. That is why some of the most successful inventors, designers, and architects are dyslexic. There are countless examples of this in virtually every industry, from fashion to movies, household products to motor vehicles, and engineers to architects.

Sir James Dyson, the British inventor, is a good example. He understood that the cyclone principle seen in a lumber mill could also be used in a vacuum cleaner. This meant that the suction would not be weakened as it fills up. This discovery enabled Dyson and his company to manufacture a bagless vacuum cleaner and subsequently many other products in everyday use throughout the world. Similarly, architect Richard Rogers turned the Pompidou Centre in Paris "inside out" by placing functional elements of the building—plumbing, electrical, ventilation, and escalators—on the outside. When people said that something was impossible, he said, "I should not believe them!" A good example of enhanced spatial awareness skills can be seen in Sir Jackie Stewart, winner of three World Drivers' Championships. He was diagnosed with dyslexia at 42 and was instrumental in implementing adaptations to race cars that increased safety. He also had a dogged determination and resilience that you often see in people with dyslexia.

INSTRUCTIONS: Be an inventor or innovator! Following are some everyday items. Try to reinvent them for another purpose, make them safer, or improve them in another way.

running shoe	
watering can	
stepladder	
backpack	
bicycle	
baby stroller	

Have you ever thought of something you can invent, like a battery-operated suitcase? Try to think of something that you've found inconvenient—anything at all! And think what you might invent to improve it. (James Dyson invented the bagless vacuum cleaner because he found it tedious to change the vacuum bag. And he was always disappointed by the low level of suction!)

VISUALIZE THE WORD/SENTENCE

Best for: practicing visualization, creative thinking

This activity will develop your visualization skills, which can help you in many different ways: in your work, with your memory, and in your personal life.

Visualization is a powerful tool. People with dyslexia usually have very powerful visual skills and often understand information more easily if it is presented visually. Visualization tends to be a right hemisphere skill, and that right hemisphere is usually seen as dominant for people with dyslexia. Visualization can help people with dyslexia think, understand, and retain information more easily than if it was written. The more they practice visualization, the more proficient they can become at it. For many people, it can be quite challenging, but it can also be fun.

INSTRUCTIONS: Make visual images of the words in the following table. For example, the steps you may follow are:

1. Look at the word and make sure you have read it correctly.

2. Close your eyes and say the word to yourself.

3. Think of an image you can associate with that word.

4. Make the image come alive by visualizing an event concerning the image. For example, if the word is *green*, you might think of grass and then cows grazing on the grass.

5. Describe the image in words, make your own drawing of the image, or both.

WORD	IMAGE
yellow	
headache	
happiness	
astute	
pinnacle	
challenge	
delight	

POINTS OF VIEW

Best for: articulating thoughts, developing vocabulary, evaluating opinions

This activity will help you consider different viewpoints, evaluate them, and develop them in writing, as well help you make difficult decisions.

Quite often people with dyslexia can debate well. They may have a different angle from others or introduce a topic in an unusual manner. Debates are often formed from shared opinions. This form of communication skill can be a strength in people with dyslexia. The main purpose of this exercise is to give you an opportunity to debate with yourself or with others if you are doing this in a group.

INSTRUCTIONS: Fill in the second and third columns for each of the statements in the following table.

STATEMENT	ARGUMENT FOR	ARGUMENT AGAINST
We should take astrology more seriously.		
History is crucial, and we all need to continuously educate ourselves about it.		
Every road should have a bike lane for cyclists.		
Public transportation should be free.		
Social media has improved human communication.		

(continued)

STATEMENT	ARGUMENT FOR	ARGUMENT AGAINST
We should be chlorinating the water supply.		
Climate change is the biggest threat to humanity.		
All people should be vegetarians.		
Smoking should be banned in all public places.		

MAKE YOUR OWN STRATEGY GAME

Best for: imagination, decision-making

This activity will help you get the most out of games. Games can be a great pastime, but also a learning and a strength-building tool!

Games are usually fun and often visual. There are lots of online games, such as solitaire, crossword puzzles, sudoku, word quests, jigsaw puzzles, and picture completions. Sometimes just showing the eyes of a movie star is enough for some people to determine the person's name. There are also block puzzles that can be fascinating, like a Rubik's Cube. Playing games and solving puzzles are ways of thinking through dilemmas and coming to decisions.

INSTRUCTIONS: Search online for brain puzzles and games to spark ideas, and then create your own game!

To get you started, here is an example strategy game. Imagine you have to get from A to B, but there are obstacles in the way, and you must make decisions about how to overcome them.

These obstacles could be things such as a phone call from another friend who desperately wants to see you now but won't move from their location, or a snowstorm that's making it difficult to see the road. What do you say? What do you do? How will you reach your destination, and what will it cost you—not in dollars but in other resources?

FASHION FIRST

This activity can help you develop your creative side, even if you think you don't have one!

Many adults with dyslexia can be creative and inventive. These attributes can apply to people in all walks of life, including the fashion industry. One of the most famous is Tommy Hilfiger, who is one of the world's premier fashion designers. He still struggles with dyslexia: "I still have trouble reading. I have to concentrate very hard at going left to right, left to right, otherwise my eye just wanders to the bottom of the page." Tommy, however, also credits his dyslexia for his success in the fashion industry. In this competitive industry, he thought differently from other designers, and his brand stood out. His dyslexia was transformed from an initial disadvantage to a clear advantage.

You don't have to be able to draw or be a great artist to be a designer. You can use other strengths: imagination, creativity, and the ability to think differently, all strong suits of people with dyslexia. You can also call on your power of observation to have a sense of current fashion trends.

INSTRUCTIONS: Part 1. Using the following scenarios, either draw or describe in writing the outfit you would create. Include as many details as possible.

An elegant dinner party

Drinks after work

Bowling

Night at the movies

Lounging at home

Dinner date

INSTRUCTIONS: Part 2. Imagine that you want to start a fashion business. Think of important points you need to consider. I'll start you off.

1. Who is the target market?

2. _____

3. _____

4. _____

5. _____

BE A PICASSO

Best for: visual imagery, creativity

This activity will help develop your visual, perceptual, and drawing skills in a nonthreatening way!

You may be very visual, but you may also think you cannot draw. However, your dyslexia may give you an advantage! For example, Pablo Picasso, who was dyslexic, was described by his teachers as "having difficulty differentiating the orientation of letters." Picasso painted his subjects as he saw them—sometimes out of order, backward, or upside down. His dyslexia obviously influenced his famous artwork, and his paintings revealed the power of imagination, so much so that he and artist Georges Braque became the founders of the Cubism art movement.

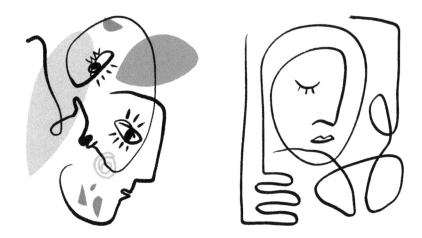

INSTRUCTIONS: In this exercise, you'll use your own power of imagination and call on your inner artist. Select any image that interests you. It can be a person, any animal, a car, an item in your home—virtually anything. Try to imagine an unusual version of the image. As an additional exercise, try to draw your unusual version to develop another one of the strengths of being dyslexic—that is, seeing the unseen!

SPATIAL THINKING AND SPATIAL TALK

Best for: strengthening visual-spatial ability, abstract thinking, vocabulary

This exercise can help you be more specific when providing directions. It will also help you increase your vocabulary!

USING SPATIAL VOCABULARY

People with dyslexia tend to be strong in spatial intelligence. That's why many enter professions that include design and engineering and that rely on visual skills, like advertising. This exercise can help you build on your existing strength in spatial intelligence.

Some studies indicate that using a wide variety of spatial vocabulary increases spatial intelligence. This means that instead of using the words *here* and *there* in your everyday language, you can try to be more specific in spatial descriptions, such as *the third street on the left just east of the town hall*. Using this kind of precise spatial language can help you visualize the spaces and shapes in order to describe them to others.

INSTRUCTIONS: Choose a place you can visualize and explain to someone where it's located, using the language of spatial intelligence. I've started you off with the town hall example.

Try to make your sentences simple and direct. Your drawings don't have to be works of art, just simple diagrams showing that you understand the meaning of the words.

WORD	SENTENCE	DIAGRAM
across	The town hall is across from the Curzon Theater.	Draw a picture here of town hall and opposite, draw the theater.
parallel to		

(continued)

WORD	SENTENCE	DIAGRAM
beyond		
to the right of		
tandem		

STATES, ABBREVIATIONS, AND FLAGS

Best for: investigating, memory, visual representation

This activity can help you develop skills in fact-finding and general knowledge.

People with dyslexia are skilled at investigation and finding things out. They can also have skills in visual representation. This exercise will draw on these skills, as it involves both investigation and drawing. Flags are tricky to draw as many of them look alike. You can test yourself with this by looking at a flag and then trying to draw it!

INSTRUCTIONS: For this challenge, follow these steps.

1. Look at each state's abbreviation and fill in the state's full name.

2. Find the flag for the state. (*Hint:* Go online and search for "U.S. state flags.")

3. Look at the flag for about 10 to 20 seconds. Then look away and try to draw it in the table.

4. As you progress through all the states, you'll likely find it easier to draw the flags. (Don't be disheartened if your flags aren't perfect! Creating a representation is still good practice.)

5. For a greater investigation challenge, try to find out the name of the singer or group famous for each song. (*Hint:* The song is in some way associated with the state. You can search for "famous songs from _____.")

For added fun, practice your drawing some more and sing along as you go!

ABBREVIATION	STATE	DRAW THE FLAG	FAMOUS SONG	SINGER/GROUP
AR			"Mary Queen of _____"	
IN			"Small Town"	
KS			"Wichita Lineman"	
LA			"House of the Rising Sun"	
MN			"Say Shh"	

(continued)

ABBREVIATION	STATE	DRAW THE FLAG	FAMOUS SONG	SINGER/GROUP
NE			"Omaha"	
NJ			"_____ Girl"	
NM			"Albuquerque"	
NV			"Waking Up in Vegas"	
SC			"Hickory Wind"	
UT			"Salt Lake City"	
WV			"Take Me Home, Country Roads"	

CHAPTER SEVEN

ADULT DYSLEXIA IN THE REAL WORLD

This chapter will focus on real-life scenarios that depict people with dyslexia using various strategies and employing their strengths to overcome challenges and excel in their professional and personal lives.

My aim is to highlight that you can overcome any challenge and reach any goal if you have the interest and motivation to succeed.

From a work perspective, there are clearly some occupations that are a better fit than others for people with dyslexia. But there are no rules governing this, and you'll find people with dyslexia in almost all professions. It's important to always be aware of your strengths when deciding on a career or job change and to use them to your advantage.

If you're in an occupation that plays to your strengths as a dyslexic person, then this is ideal. You'll find many examples of people who have succeeded because they've been able to use their strengths. Some of these will be highlighted in this chapter.

Irrespective of your profession, you may still find some work tasks challenging, and you may be confronted with obstacles. You can, however, overcome them, and one of the goals of this chapter is to show some of the ways others have done this in relatable situations.

The same holds true in your personal life. Whether you have daily organizational and time-management hurdles that cause great stress and prevent you from enjoying life, or challenges reaching long-term goals, always focus on your strengths and know it's possible to learn the skills and employ effective strategies to reach your idea of success and personal satisfaction.

You are not alone. Many people, with or without dyslexia, can find some work tasks challenging and have difficulties in their personal lives. Your dyslexia may even give you advantages, like the ability to think outside the box and to use a visual and random thinking style that may well elude others. In short, you can excel with dyslexia.

Each of the real-life scenarios and solutions will show how an adult with dyslexia who is facing an obstacle in their work or personal life can overcome it. I will also highlight how to use a strength to your advantage. Some of the obstacles we'll discuss are:

* Time management

* Attention to detail

* Memorization

* Organization

* Concentration/focus

* Low self-esteem

* Stress

The strengths that will also be highlighted include:

* Imagination, creativity, and curiosity

* Abstract thinking

* Thinking outside the box

* Spatial reasoning and visualizing three-dimensionally

In Real Life: Dana's Time and Task Management

Dana worked as an administrator in a busy office and often became flustered at the number and variety of tasks she had to carry out in a day. One of her challenges as someone with dyslexia related to time management and carrying out all the tasks she had been allocated for that day. Invariably she had to stay after work hours to complete these and often took work home with her. Dana was aware that some other administrators were able to complete their tasks during the workday. This caused her frustration and anxiety. Dana understood her work and responsibilities, and she had good verbal skills—she could identify key points in discussions, and she was able to respond to telephone queries well by using this strength.

Strategy: Prioritize, Plan, and Reflect

- **Prioritize**

  » Dana wrote down all the tasks she wished to achieve in the day. She numbered them 1 to 4 (1 being the most important and 4 the least important). In addition to numbering them, she decided to color-code them (1 = green, 2 = orange, 3 = red, 4 = blue). This gave her a way to estimate the amount of time she might need for each of the tasks.

- **Plan**

  » She then worked out when she wanted to carry out the priority tasks. She identified four priority tasks and then colored these using the same coding system she used previously.

- **Reflect**

  » After she completed the tasks, she focused on questions such as "Did I complete all the tasks?" "Could I have used my time more efficiently?" "What were my distracters?" and "Is there another way I can deal with them moving forward?"

The Outcome

One of the purposes of this plan was to help Dana develop her own time-management plan. She learned what her distracters were and how she could deal with them. Implementing the new strategies helped Dana assume significantly more control over her own learning and the development of her own personal strategies. This made her more independent, which is important for all people with dyslexia, and it is important to try to adapt this strategy to your own personal and work experiences.

In Real Life: Jerry's Reading Speed

Jerry's career was always related to technology, and he had a good inside knowledge of how technology works. At 51 years old, he was very experienced in all aspects of computer work. He progressed well in the company where he works but found in his promoted position that he has to process written information very quickly and make almost instant decisions.

Jerry was diagnosed with dyslexia in his mid-40s, and he always had difficulties with reading speed. His assessment showed that his oral language comprehension was in the top 1 percent for his age range, and his visual abilities were also very high. His reading speed, however, was low. Although he was able to read reasonably accurately, he required a great deal of time. His new position with the company included reading and writing reports at speed, as well as giving presentations. He found these aspects of his work very challenging and he began to feel frustrated and embarrassed.

Strategy: Facilitating Discussion and Creativity

- Jerry had reading speed difficulties, so the reports he had to read at speed were transferred to audio mode.

- He had excellent oral language comprehension, so Jerry asked his employers for more opportunities to discuss the reports before and after he read them.

- He also had excellent abstract thinking skills, which meant that he often came up with ideas that others had not thought of. Of course, this impressed his employers.

- His employers arranged a course for him in scanning and skimming.

- One of the most important factors to help with the obstacles was to allow Jerry to use his abstract thinking skills, creativity, and out-the-box way of thinking. His task was changed so he did not have to report or summarize the documents. Instead, he was presented with questions relating to implementing innovative ways of working based on the documents and follow-up ideas.

The Outcome

As expected, Jerry thrived when given work priorities that allowed space for creativity, use of self-initiative, and computer work. Additionally, he was able to access assistive technology to help with reading. He also used some strategies to help with skimming and scanning, such as working out in advance what he needed to obtain from a text, taking notes, and color-coding the key points.

Jerry's frustration and embarrassment levels diminished. His management became more sensitive to his needs and to dyslexia and ensured he was not overexposed to potentially vulnerable situations.

SPOTLIGHT: RICHARD BRANSON, ENTREPRENEUR

Richard Branson is an excellent advocate for supporting people with dyslexia. He is happy to claim that his dyslexia is at least partially responsible for his success. His creativity and imagination may well have been the keys to the success of the Virgin Group. He also suggests that people with dyslexia can have the skills needed for the future of the workplace. He says jobs that include problem-solving, creativity, and imagination—jobs that are tailor-made for people with dyslexia—will proliferate with the rise of artificial intelligence (AI) and automation.

In Real Life: Carla's Memory Missteps

Carla was a CEO in an expanding and successful international pharmaceutical company. She had achieved a great number of qualifications, had superb product knowledge, and had worked for the same company since her doctoral graduation. She had astute decision-making skills but found challenges in reading comprehension, remembering statistics, and recalling the names and designations of people in the company.

Although she had a relaxed communication style, she was quite anxious about the responsibilities of her role and specifically remembering the names and responsibilities of the individuals in the project teams in the key areas of the company. She was made CEO because of her excellent decision-making skills and knowledge of the company. There had been sweeping internal changes and many staff changes since her promotion. She was often called upon to give press interviews and oral reports to the board and shareholders. She would become flustered by the number of new projects and the expectations of the audience.

Strategy: Acronyms and Visuals

- Carla had an excellent visual memory and was particularly skilled in visualizing three-dimensionally. We decided that she should have a photograph of the heads and deputy heads of all departments and projects with the person's name printed at the bottom of each photo.

- She suggested that in addition to a still shot, she should have a photo of each of them doing something characteristic, such as playing football, looking at a fashion magazine, reading, or shrugging shoulders.

- Carla also formulated standard criteria for project, determining that:

  » Each project should have a unique acronym, and this should be attached to a photo of the project head.

  » Each project head had to submit a mind map (see chapter 4) of the project, including future directions and written reports.

  » Each project report should be memory-friendly and include a checklist that would clearly indicate in bullet point form the aims, achievements, future work, and expected completion date.

The Outcome

The proposals were put into practice, and Carla was able to associate the photos with the name and the project. The acronym helped her remember the name of the project, and the bullet point lists made for quick and easy responses to questions. Carla made up her own mind map based on the way this information was presented. This meant she created her own organization of the information she had to remember. The act of doing this helped her retain and recall the information more readily because she had done it her way! She even began using this strategy for aspects of her personal life, such as remembering things on a grocery list.

In Real Life: Crystal's Literacy and Memory Obstacles

Crystal was a committed and popular music teacher diagnosed with dyslexia as an adult. She was very creative and could learn and play music by ear. She had been a music teacher for 15 years, but she still had difficulties reading and remembering musical scores and would often forget song lyrics. She over-relied on her ear for music. In the assessment the psychologist carried out, her visual processing and language comprehension were very high. Her short- and long-term memory, however, were both below average. Her reading accuracy, speed, and comprehension were all low. She had excellent imaginative skills, but her written work lacked structure and organization.

Strategy: Prepare to Remember

Crystal was aware of the issues that could be obstacles when teaching. Since she was aware of these, she was able to plan and prepare in advance. Crystal could:

- Have a template of the music score she would be using in that lesson and use color for the different notes, ensuring that there is wide spacing between the lines on the staff. The rhythms can be visually marked with lines or colors to show the main beats.

- Have any lyrics printed in large type with double spacing prior to the lesson.

- Take care when using of the terms *right hand* and *left hand* and also with *higher* or *lower* in relation to the instruments. She could highlight these ahead of time.

- Make a list of music equipment required for the lesson.

The Outcome

The larger-type music score with extra spacing helped with sequencing, as Crystal was in the habit of missing lines, which used to cause some good-humored hilarity in the classroom. The colored notes helped with tracking and the differentiation between notes. She was able to focus the lesson on the individual children and their specific needs. Overall, she felt more confident and did not fear making any glaring mistakes. She was also supported by the knowledge that many famous and successful musicians are dyslexic, including Cher, Ozzy Osbourne, Mick Fleetwood, Gwen Stefani, Jewel, and Tony Bennett.

In Real Life: David's Reading, Writing, and Number Issues

David was a sales assistant in a small hardware store. Since the company was small, he was given duties beyond selling over the counter. His work, in fact, involved a wide range of activities relating to warehousing tasks, store inventory, deliveries, and administrative tasks.

David has had long-standing difficulties with reading, writing, and number work, and he was diagnosed with dyslexia while in school. He described his strengths as the ability to work things out visually, excellent spatial reasoning skills, and three-dimensional visualization skills.

Since his duties involved reading lists and writing up daily reports based on the store inventory, he found he had to work late just to complete that day's work. He indicated that time management was his greatest challenge, as he was unable to read and write quickly. He often had to reread and was constantly checking over his spelling. He did find that using audio software on the computer helped, as did spell-check, but he still had time-management and organizational issues.

Strategy: Monthly Plan to Prioritize

David discussed his problems with his manager. This can be a good option, as it can form the basis of trust and subsequent support. They determined that David had too many duties to perform in the week, and it was little wonder that time management was a big issue. The meeting was constructive, and they made a number of decisions to help David work more efficiently each month.

- David should allocate a week when he would prioritize deliveries. If he had any free time during that week, he should take one type of item from the store (e.g., assembly tools) and take a stock count of that item. During that week, he would be relieved of counter duties.

- The following week would be counter work in the mornings and deliveries in the afternoons.

- The third week of the month would be allocated to counter work in the mornings and administration in the afternoons.

- For the fourth week, David would meet with his line manager on Monday morning, and together they would decide what they would prioritize that week. If there were a large amount of deliveries to complete, he would prioritize those.

- David has good visual-spatial skills and was able to make a visual plan that would be more meaningful to him and understandable at a glance.

The Outcome

A mutual feeling of openness and trust developed between David and his manager. David felt he was an important member of the staff and that he could call on his boss for advice without feeling like a failure due to the challenges from dyslexia. This was a problem David had experienced at school, where he felt inadequate for asking questions when the answers seemed to be obvious to others. David therefore had become reluctant to open up about any difficulties he was experiencing.

His working month was now well planned, and it was organized in a way that was very manageable. Additionally, there was further scope for discussion during the fourth week of the month to ensure that David did not fall behind in any area of his work.

SPOTLIGHT: RICHARD FORD, AUTHOR

Acclaimed novelist Richard Ford won the Pulitzer Prize in 1996 for his novel *Independence Day*. He says that he did not read a book until he was 19 and that he's still a slow reader. To address challenges with dyslexia, he devises very detailed clerical procedures and works at his own pace. He feels he has learned to cope with his dyslexia because he has developed a writing and reading lifestyle. There are many budding authors who are dyslexic, and it's motivating to read about successful authors who have persevered and overcome some of the barriers associated with dyslexia.

In Real Life: Vera's Artistic Side

Vera had not always been successful, but she had always been artistic. Being dyslexic, she had long-standing difficulties with pronunciation, particularly multisyllabic words. She felt embarrassed by this and often laughed it off, and people saw her as a fun-loving person. But she wanted to be treated seriously as an artist. Her dyslexic pattern of thinking, which was essentially in pictures, contributed to her creativity. She always enjoyed creative pursuits.

She knew she had talent, and she was also aware that many people with dyslexia have artistic talents. In the feedback she received after she was diagnosed with dyslexia, the psychologist mentioned her artistic talents and also told her that she scored very high in all the visual subtests. Although this gave her confidence, her creativity was not acknowledged at school, and she was directed toward a job in the hotel industry. She found everything prescribed for her, and the work was very routine. This was her biggest turn-off. Although she was a polite and pleasant person, she was honest when she said that her lack of motivation was unfortunately obvious to her bosses. She tried to hide this from the customers. It slowly occurred to her that the actual environment was predictable and uninspiring. Every room in the hotel was the same—even the pictures and artwork.

Strategy: Perseverance and Creativity

Vera had not specialized yet in any form of art, but she could turn her hand to most things—glass, drawing, and interior decoration. She has excellent visual-spatial skills and can easily work in three dimensions. She received permission from her manager to come into the hotel on some of her free workdays, observe the hotel environment, and suggest some changes. This was a bold move on her part, and her manager, although cooperative, did not feel it was going to lead to anything significant.

Vera felt that the hotel should be different from what people might expect. The unexpected can often be interesting and appealing. Drawing on her creativity, Vera suggested the following:

- The foyer/lobby should have a showpiece artist of the month and obtain pieces from local artists for display.

- On Fridays, the desk and lobby staff should have a dress as you like day (within reason!).

- They should put different-colored light bulbs in the lamps on the side tables and create a different ambience in the evening as opposed to the day.

The Outcome

Vera felt that she was using her creativity and that this was being acknowledged by the management.

Her self-esteem increased, and so did her job satisfaction, even though she was still doing the same job. The management listened to her and eventually offered her a position in the design department in the hotel chain. The message of this scenario is "stick with it." Cherish and nourish your skills and strong suits, even though you may not always be able to use them. As Picasso said, "Art washes from the soul the dust of everyday life."

In Real Life: Josh's Low Self-Esteem

When Josh was diagnosed with dyslexia, he recalled his head teacher at school remarking that he would go nowhere unless he improved his grades drastically. Josh felt it was those negative comments that spurred him on and made him strive to acquire a good career. He recalls that when he left school, he had to undertake a course in basic skills before he could continue with his education. He went on to a career as a mechanical designer mainly working with machines.

Josh liked working with machines because they provided a multiperceptual experience—he could feel, see, and experience what he was working on. As a result, he saw products in different dimensions by using different modalities. While content with his work performance, he still felt the effects of low self-esteem that had started with his teacher's remarks back in school. Everyday life events could sometimes be traumatic and stressful for him.

Strategy: Use Strengths, Focus on Relaxation, Build Self-Confidence

- Josh's employer understood that people with dyslexia can have many strengths. His employer encouraged Josh to talk openly in formal staff meetings about his dyslexia and how he was able to use the strengths that stem from it.

- Josh watched a video about mindfulness and started practicing a relaxation regime that involved some meditation.

- He also started attending a yoga class with a friend.

- He realized he was strong in the visual area and started to attend a woodworking class once weekly in the evening.

The Outcome

After opening up about his dyslexia and the many strengths it brought him, Josh really appreciated being supported and feeling successful professionally. This helped him cope with other personal and stressful matters. His colleagues learned a lot about multisensory activities, and Josh was happy to help other people understand dyslexia, particularly those who were parents of children with dyslexia.

Meanwhile, his mindfulness regime helped to clear his mind of issues he was harboring from the past. Practicing yoga helped him wind down. He found the 10-minute relaxation at the end of each class very relaxing, and it seemed to remove much of the tension he experienced from everyday life events. His woodworking teacher highly praised his work, which boosted Josh's self-esteem. The atmosphere at the class was relaxed and nonthreatening—very much the opposite from what he'd experienced during his earlier years at school. This helped to reverse the negative feelings he had about school and put things into perspective. This scenario emphasizes the importance of working within your comfort zone. This can help you identify and use your strengths.

SPOTLIGHT: HENRY WINKLER, ACTOR

Widely known for his portrayal of "The Fonz" on *Happy Days*, Henry Winkler didn't read his first book until he was 31. He was thought of as lazy at school, and he says he was grounded for most of his high school years. His strategy was to memorize and think on his feet.

Success in acting made him more confident and inspired him to help others facing the same self-doubt he'd experienced. He's collaborated with Lin Oliver and written a series of children's books centering on the life of Hank Zipzer, a fourth-grade boy who has trouble reading.

In Real Life: Fatima's Organizational Skills

Fatima was always interested in literature and had a real ambition to become a librarian. Although she was dyslexic, her reading had improved considerably, and by the time she graduated from high school, she was reading well and had excellent abstract thinking skills. But she was still frustrated by a number of dyslexia issues. Her organization was, in her own words, "nonexistent," and her written work needed several rounds of proofreading.

Fatima did achieve her ambition of becoming a librarian, and through a great deal of hard work managed to secure a job in an international financial and law company working in the archives department. She soon picked up the language of the company, and her knowledge of the archive material was impressive. But she had a real difficulty creating an ordered system for her archive data. Although some of the data was electronic, some of the less recent material and some sensitive material were kept in the archive store. Fatima decided to seek some assistance with organization after management indicated that she had to improve in this area, as retrieving archives quickly was vital.

Strategy: Organization Plan

- Fatima realized that filing by date order was not sufficient, as archives were often requested by name or topic.

- In conjunction with her manager, she noted all the major topics that the company was involved in.

- She made heading cards that she inserted at intervals in the archive filing room.

- For each topic, she then made separate divider cards for months and year.

The Outcome

By going through this process, Fatima was able to retrieve the information by topic much more easily, particularly when the senior company managers were on an international video call and information was requested unexpectedly. It also helped Fatima gain more knowledge about the different areas of the company, as she had to be aware of the varied topics/areas in which the company was involved. The process additionally aided her with the filing of electronic archives. Her quick retrieval and efficiency impressed the management, and Fatima was soon rewarded with a promotion.

In Real Life: Elijah's Directional Hurdles

Elijah always wanted to join the US Army, and not too long after his training, he was promoted to private first class. During basic combat training, his corporal was impressed with his speed at carrying out instructions and his attitude on the job. Elijah had disclosed his dyslexia when he'd initially enlisted, and it hadn't been a problem. However, Elijah knew he had a weakness that so far no one had picked up on. He still had difficulty with directions: left and right, but also behind and before. And when a time reference was used in directions, he really had to keep his wits about him. Elijah was hoping to eventually be promoted, but this meant he would have to give orders to others.

Strategy: Practice to Make It Second Nature

- Elijah was left-handed, and he was dominant on his left side. He related left to his dominant side, so he did not have to think what was left or right. If left was the instruction, he just moved toward his dominant side.

- He practiced this when he was on his own, using headphones to listen to a tape he'd made himself.

- He also put some location directions on the tape that he found challenging to respond to, such as *behind*, *after*, *around*, *next to*, *on*, and *between*. He found himself a quiet outdoor space, such as a park, and he played the phrases. He kept practicing until he was able to respond correctly and automatically.

- For the time directions, he did the same. He found an open space and listened to prerecorded directions, such as "Walk to 3 o'clock," etc., practicing until he was also able to do these automatically.

The Outcome

With all of his practice, Elijah was able to do everything automatically without thinking about it. It became second nature to him, and he felt confident in carrying out the instructions correctly. He was than able to focus on other areas of his job and excel.

SPOTLIGHT: JENNIFER ANISTON, ACTOR

Jennifer Aniston, like so many adults with dyslexia, didn't find out she was dyslexic until she was in her 20s, and like so many others, obtaining that diagnosis helped change her thinking about her abilities. Now there was a reason she had so many challenges at school and why she chose the role of class clown over teacher's pet!

In Real Life: Maya's Report Writing

Maya had just qualified as an accountant and was very happy to land a position with an enterprising company in the town where she lived. She was excellent with numbers, but being dyslexic, she had difficulties writing reports and responding to emails. The company was happy with how she was able to prepare accounts, but she experienced real problems when it came to reporting on monthly and quarterly accounts. This involved more than presenting numbers. It included making projections and reporting on competitors. This caused Maya a great deal of anxiety.

Strategy: Reorganize, Prioritize, Summarize

- Maya had been mixing accounting tables and prose in her reports, which made them rather jumbled. We decided that all the tables would go into an appendix at the end and be numbered alphabetically. This meant she could focus on the actual written reports.

- She created an introduction, a table of contents, and a main body that she organized under two headings: "Achievements" and "Proposal Projections."

- She summarized these, and if she wanted to go into more detail, she numbered those details in a separate paper. For example, she might say, "See paper 1."

- Her reports now contained an introduction with contents, a main body, concluding comments, additional numbered papers, and supporting tables, each alphabetically annotated.

- She also made a report template to help her with future reports.

The Outcome

Using this structure, Maya was able to complete the reports faster and to present them in a more accessible format. At meetings when she had to talk about a report, she found it easier to refer people to the appropriate part of the report. Maya was also able to use this system with other similar tasks.

In Real Life: Amos's Presentation Pitfalls

Amos was a popular landscape architect who'd helped design a number of new public parks and residential neighborhoods. He'd been complimented on his awareness of the environment; he had superb visual-spatial skills; and he always prioritized ample flowers, shrubs, and trees, as well as water features in the areas he planned.

But Amos's dyslexia meant it was challenging for him to make public presentations. He had a word-finding problem, which is quite common in dyslexia, and he sometimes used the wrong word when talking in public. He also found it very stressful to respond to questions at open public meetings.

Strategy: Implement Presentation Best Practices

- It was important for Amos to ensure that a data projector was available and to make his presentation in PowerPoint or a similar visual medium.

- He would organize the slides to:

  » Identify the purpose of the project in the first slide

  » Give details of the project under suitable headings

  » Illustrate his points with visuals

  » Conclude with who would benefit from the completed project and why

  » Present some questions on the last slide that he expected people would want answered

  » Answer anticipated questions in advance

- He would then feel more confident and more able to take live questions from the audience.

- If he didn't know the answer or was unsure how to put it in words, he could say that he would find out and inform people through email. Alternatively, he could take one question during the presentation and ask people to stay behind if they had any other pressing questions.

- He needed to ensure that he avoided confrontation and unnecessary digression and that he remained polite, understanding, and sincere.

The Outcome

Amos became more confident in presenting, and he found that many of the questions being asked by audiences were similar. He became more succinct and more relevant in his responses.

In Real Life: Marty's Forgetfulness

Marty was a civil engineer who contributed to many important projects, such as new highways, bridges, and a new airport. Although he was astute at problem-solving and decision-making and was a valuable member of the team, he had difficulties with memory. Often, colleagues had to remind him of a formula or a task he still had to do. He was good at the big picture, and that impressed colleagues a great deal. However, Marty was embarrassed by his forgetfulness and wanted to access some support for it.

Marty ticked all the boxes for being a civil engineer. He was creative and good at problem-solving, understood the bigger picture of a project, could think three-dimensionally, and was a good communicator, but he felt his memory was his downfall.

Strategy: Mind Mapping, Reminders, Reviewing

- Marty took stock and worked out the areas where he felt memory was an issue. He found these included scheduling appointments, following up on appointments, noting any revisions to plans, remembering people's names from previous projects, and figuring the time scale of a project. Fortunately, he worked as part of a team, so he could rely on others to ensure that he remembered those points.

- Marty wanted to improve his memory in general, as well as for specific aspects of his work. He talked to his boss, and they realized it was important to tackle this, so he implemented a powerful technique to develop memory skills.

- Marty immediately started to use mind mapping to remember the names and the progress of projects.

- He also used prompts for meetings so that an alert sounded on his laptop 10 minutes before a meeting.

- He applied an active learning mechanism to strengthen experiential memory by spending 30 minutes at the end of each day reviewing the work he'd done that day and any follow-up that was necessary.

The Outcome

By consciously tackling his memory issues, Marty implemented the strategies best suited to him, and he gained confidence from doing it. He felt that he had relied on colleagues quite a lot, but this was okay as they were always willing to help. However, he obtained a sense of achievement by developing his own memory strategies. This gave him a new confidence to further develop memory strategies and to try out new ways of retaining information.

Sir Jackie Stewart is a three-time Formula One world champion. The iconic worldwide figure has used his talents in many ways. A relentless advocate for children and adults with dyslexia, he is also an inspiring speaker and a good example of how people with dyslexia can use their strengths not only to help themselves deal with dyslexia but also to help others. Sir Jackie has used his strengths and has shown a real determination of purpose, which is shared by many people with dyslexia. Throughout his life he's been a staunch advocate of developing safety in Formula One racing. He's pursued many goals in the field of dyslexia, from supporting teacher training to early assessment to inspiring adults to be all they can be. A true champion!

In Real Life: Tammy's Memory Issue

Tammy was a part-time yoga teacher as well as a part-time pharmacy assistant. She hoped to return to school in the near future to take university courses to become an industrial chemist. At school she excelled in team sports. Being very athletic and interested in yoga, she took a number of intensive courses to become a yoga teacher. She was good at displaying the various yoga positions but found that when she was running a class on her own, she forgot the sequence of the different positions she'd intended to do. This meant there were often pauses in the classes while she referred to her notes. Yoga is supposed to be natural and spontaneous, and although some yoga teachers do refer to notes, Tammy knew she had difficulties with sequencing due to her dyslexia and felt she wanted to conduct the class without referencing notes.

Strategy: Visual Aids

- Tammy worked out that in most lessons she would use six main positions. Each of those positions had subpositions that help yoga practitioners get into the main position, but these were self-explanatory and followed a logical yoga sequence.

- Tammy made large line drawings, or made copies of the line drawings from her yoga manual, of the positions she intended using in that class.

- She pinned them on the wall in the order she was going to teach them.

- She made no secret of this, as she said it would also help the class to see and review the positions they had done during that class.

- She introduced the positions they were going to be doing, directing students to the posted drawings. The names of the positions (for example, mountain pose) were in large, bold font so Tammy was able to see them at a glance.

- She encouraged the class to take a photo of the drawings so they could practice the yoga positions at home.

The Outcome

Tammy's yoga class was able to flow well, and she felt more confident. Many people with dyslexia have issues with sequencing, and it's important that they use problem-solving, which can be a real strength for people with dyslexia. Tammy was able to use her problem-solving skills to implement strategies that effect change. Doing this boosted her confidence! Tammy found she was able to relax when she got home after class.

In Real Life: Joe's Daily Forgetfulness and Stress

For Joe, dyslexia was not only a challenge at work but also an integral part of his everyday life. He believed it impacted him more in his personal life than in the workplace. Most days, Joe's inner thoughts were riddled with questions: *Where did I put my car keys? Where did I put that note with the groceries I have to pick up today? What time is the parents' meeting at school tonight? Is it this weekend the Sinclairs are coming for dinner? Do I still have to email Mike about that meeting? How do I always start with so much time but always feels rushed at the end of the day?*

Living with dyslexia presented ongoing challenges, and Joe knew these challenges were a problem. But he was always too busy and often too stressed to sit down and work out a strategy. Things finally got out of hand due to his forgetfulness of important dates, events, and other items. A crisis became his catalyst for change. Joe sat down with a counselor and worked on making changes.

Strategy: Use Technology, Prioritize, Establish Routines

- Joe needed to make full use of available technology. All appointments could be recorded electronically, with a pop-up reminder 30 minutes before an appointment. He applied an active learning strategy to strengthen his memory. At the end of each day, Joe spent 30 minutes reviewing the work he'd done that day and noted any follow-up that was necessary.

- His wife would take full responsibility for arranging the family outings and occasions when Joe had a busy time at work.

- He prioritized activities into "must do" and "can wait." Every week he reviewed the "can waits" and worked out when he would do these.

- He would try to have a routine for leisure and social occasions, so he'd allocate specific days and evenings for each. If he designated a certain block of free time, it would remain that way except for extreme circumstances.

- Joe established a daily routine and stuck to it. This helped him become more efficient and ultimately less stressed. He had to designate times and days for his activities, social time, and family life. As a memory aid, he made a chart of his weekly routine and posted it on the fridge.

The Outcome

Joe became more confident in addressing the issues that arose from his dyslexia and in taking responsibility for dealing with it. Acceptance leads to action, and action can lead to success and reassurance. He also felt less stressed and better able to remember everything, ultimately enjoying his personal time with friends, family, and himself much more.

Conclusion

I would very much like to congratulate you on completing this workbook. I hope it has helped you reshape your thinking about dyslexia and its potential impact. I particularly hope that you have embraced the positive aspects of dyslexia that have been highlighted throughout this book. These are so important—I would rank having positive self-esteem as being among the most important factors for achieving personal satisfaction, however you define it. Additionally, I would like to mention self-advocacy. I hope the information in this book will help you to strive for and achieve self-advocacy in whatever you do—work and leisure. Self-advocacy represents a shift toward greater personal responsibility and more self-direction, and these can contribute to success at work and in life in general.

This book has covered a wide range of areas from reading to problem-solving and visual-spatial thinking to developing skills in writing. This is because it is important to focus on you and your individual needs. One of the aims of the book is to help you reflect on your life and the impact dyslexia has had on you, and for you to successfully manage this—hopefully aided by the activities in this book—and achieve your hopes and ambitions.

I must reiterate here that I am very aware of the strengths and the potential of people with dyslexia. The final chapter of this book is clear evidence of that. We all know that many valued innovations in society and the crucial new horizons that have been reached have been due to the endeavors and the unique skill set of individuals with dyslexia. As a society, we need to applaud that fact and stand up and support those with dyslexia. We need to nourish the talents of the young and support them as they venture through school and the workplace.

The outcome for people with dyslexia in education and at work greatly depends on people's perceptions. The book has touched on this point, and we must continue to reframe society's view of dyslexia. We are moving from the outdated idea of a disability to one that promotes equality, equity, and ability—the ability to succeed and be seen as a valued and valuable asset to the workplace and to society. You have a part to play in this, and it is my sincere hope that this book has been both a catalyst and a comfort to people with dyslexia in all walks of life.

Answer Key

CHAPTER TWO

Recipe for Spelling

s/al/t	m/ea/t	g/ar/l/i/c	b/a/s/i/l
h/a/m	n/u/t/s	m/a/ng/o	l/e/m/o/n
c/r/ea/m	s/p/r/ou/t/s	sh/r/i/m/p	m/u/sh/r/oo/m
p/ea/s	g/i/n/g/er	s/ee/d/s	oi/l
m/i/l/k	y/ea/s/t/	c/or/n	m/i/s/o
f/i/sh	b/l/ue/b/err/y	al/m/o/n/d	w/al/n/u/t
b/r/o/th	h/o/n/ey	c/el/er/y	g/r/ee/n/s

Spot the Vowel

WORDS	SHORT VOWEL	LONG VOWEL
mat	mat	
pen	Pen	
go		go
blend	blend	
text	text	
bee		bee
sea		sea

(continued)

WORDS	SHORT VOWEL	LONG VOWEL
prep	prep	
shake		shake
cry		cry
trend	trend	

Spelling: Drop the *E*

WORD	SUFFIX
drive	driving drivable
spike	spiking spiked
shame	shamed shameful shaming shameless
skate	skated skating
save	saved saving
strive	strived striving

state	stateless stated stating
postpone	postponed postponing postponement
bake	baked baking
fake	faked faking
brave	braved braving

List It: Spelling Choices

/ā/ spelled ay, ai, a_e, and a	/ch/ spelled ch and tch	/k/ spelling k, ck, and c	/f/ spelled ph and f	/j/ spelled dge	/ī/ spelled i, y, and i_e
List at least two more words that use these spellings.	List at least four more words that use these spellings.	List at least two more words that use these spellings.	List at least four more words that use these spellings.	List at least five more words that use these spellings.	List at least three more words that use these spellings.
rain	coach	king	graph	judge	fly
play	catch	duck	first	fudge	strive

(continued)

/ā/ spelled ay, ai, a_e, and a	/ch/ spelled ch and tch	/k/ spelling k, ck, and c	/f/ spelled ph and f	/j/ spelled dge	/ī/ spelled i, y, and i_e
brave	witch	camp	phoneme	dodge	tiger
paper	watch	kid	elephant	fridge	try
pain	crunch	flock	phonics	hedge	triangle
	inch		flower	badge	

Positional Spellings

dge—dodge

j—jump

ch—churn and lurch

tch—catch

ay—day

ai—nail or lain

a_e—brave

i_e—drive

y—cry

c—cut

k—kite

ck—puck

sna**ck**	str**ay**	cru**tch**	junk
fri**dge**	cr**y**	fl**y**	**p**ain
truck	ca**tch**	do**dge**	bake
kilt	pr**ay**	h**ay**	fle**ck**
li**ck**	**ch**air	bake	**k**ing
chimp	spik**e**	**ch**ick	snail
clo**ck**	bla**ck**		

Plurals: Rules and Exceptions

churches

boxes

keys

ways

losses

dishes

flies

dresses

pianos

fishes

Sentences: Sounds the Same

1. mail

2. genes

3. write

4. two

5. buy

6. stationary

7. compliment

8. course

9. peace

10. raise

Day Timer: Word Tricks

Answers will vary. Here are some examples.

address	She changed her address. The speaker addressed the audience.
bear	A wild bear can be dangerous. Extra work at this point was more than she could bear.
case	The inspector solved the case. He put his papers into his case and left.
contract	The new employee signed a contract. It was crucial that the scientist did not contract the virus.

fine	The hairdresser said she had very thin, fine hair.
	He was satisfied with the job and told the worker everything was fine.
found	He found the $20 bill on the ground.
	Bill Gates decided to found a new charity.
fudge	He enjoyed the fudge; it was his favorite treat.
	The audience knew immediately that speaker had fudged the answer and avoided the truth.
grouse	The workers were told if they wanted to grouse about the new working conditions to put their complaints in writing.
	The grouse is a large, flamboyant bird.
lead	Lead is a precious metal.
	The captain took the lead on the field.
match	The match between the tennis players ended in a draw.
	He used match after match to try to light the fire.
object	He did not like the idea and was sure to object to it.
	The hiker's view was spoiled by a large object in the distance.
pound	In some countries like Egypt and the United Kingdom, the pound is the unit of currency. He had to pound the nail into the solid piece of wood.
	He used a hammer to pound the pole into the ground.
right	The worker knew he was in the right as he had read his employment contract carefully. She decided it would be quicker to turn right at the next junction.
	In the United States, Canada, and Europe, people drive on the right side of the road.
row	He had to row quickly to beat the record time.
	I want to sit in the front row at the concert.
tender	After washing her hands vigorously, they were soft and tender.
	He went to his boss to tender his resignation.

Matching the Phrases

Democracy is viewed as beneficial 1	The work recreation room 15	Was the role of a key member of staff 10	Had many pages and took a long time to read 16
Time management 14	The work manual 8	As it helped him manage his finances 5	Reduce the blood flow around the body 4
The kitchen was fully equipped 3	The study of genes 9	Should be free 11	Was canceled because of terrible weather 13
Sedentary occupations 4	**Since everyone is able to vote 1**	The work golf outing 13	Occupied lots of space in his work van 7
Overtime was helpful 5	Reading current work reports 10	She was rewarded by her employer 2	But knew what he was capable of 12
The medical journal 6	Public transportation 11	With fridge and microwave 3	For meeting her monthly goals 2
The large tool kit 7	Includes reviews of recent clinical studies 6	Listed job duties 8	Can detect the probability of health issues 9
The health and safety information manual 16	The swimmer faced a major challenge 12	Was used by most in their free time 15	Was important because her schedule was already overbooked 14

Catchy Phrases: Idioms

at the drop of a hat = immediately

call it a day = finish

under the weather = sick

loose cannon = free spirit

CLUE	IDIOM
idealistic	pie in the sky
what someone is thinking	penny for your thoughts
a disputed issue	hot potato
to come up to expectations	cut the mustard
exactly right	hit the nail on the head
choose between two unpleasant choices	between a rock and a hard place
a problem to be avoided	elephant in the room
inexperienced, new to something	wet behind the ears
familiar with the procedure	know the drill
when a situation becomes difficult	when the chips are down

CHAPTER THREE

Is It or Isn't It?: Commonly Confused Words

COMMONLY CONFUSED WORDS	MEANING/DIFFERENCE
bazaar/bizarre	fair/unusual
dual/duel	double/contest
eminent/imminent	famous/looming, coming soon
entitle/title	allow/name, heading
exalt/exult	elevate/rejoice
flounder/founder	stumble/creator
marital/martial	married/military
moral/morale	honest/self-confidence
precedent/president	example/leader
turbid/turgid	muddled/pompous

Preposition Fun!

Answers will vary. Here are some examples.

across	She walked across the road to greet her friends.
along	The boy was walking along the edge of the lake.
at	He was waiting at the corner.
between	The apartment building was located between two parks.

down	The weary traveler sat down to rest on a rock.
from	The bird swooped from the dense bush.
off	The sign said, "Keep off the grass" in bold letters.
upon	The small bird perched upon the telephone wire.
within	The fountain was within the park.

Place *B*, *D*, *P*, and *T* in the Word

WORD	CLUE
ALPHABET	all the letters
ADAPTABLE	flexible
TRUMPET	a brass instrument
CLIPBOARD	used to write on
CUPBOARD	place for storing food
EXPENDABLE	no longer necessary
DISPOSABLE	can be thrown out
PAPERBACK	softcover book
PREDICTABLE	likely to happen
UNPERTURBED	not worried or concerned
UPGRADE	to make an improvement

(continued)

WORD	CLUE
SUBPOENAED	legally made to attend a court
PRESCRIBED	dictated
DECOMPOSABLE	can be broken down and reabsorbed
SHIPBUILDER	person who builds seaworthy vessels
PUBLICIZE	to tell everyone
PEBBLES	decorative stones
BUILDUP	collection

Practice Making Connections

Answers will vary. Here are some examples.

cappuccino	Italy/South America	the home of coffee
computer	spell-check	an important use of a computer
detergent	soap	another word to for something used to clean
economy	money	key ingredient of the economy

music	download	how music can be accessed
restaurant	menu	the first thing you receive after entering a restaurant

Why, Oh, Why?

The responses from the Internet may vary. Often there is no firm agreement on the origin of a word or phrase, so there may be different answers from those listed here.

berserk		The word berserk came into English in the early 19th century as a noun used to describe an ancient Norse warrior who fought with uncontrolled ferocity (also known as a berserker).
break the ice		Break the ice means to forge a path for others to follow. It alludes to the breaking of ice to allow the navigation of boats. The figurative use is quite old and was recorded by Sir Thomas North in his 1579 translation of Plutarch's Lives of the Noble Grecians and Romanes.

(continued)

butterfingers		Butterfingers was in use in 1615 with the same meaning we have for it today; that is, someone likely to drop things—as if their hands were smeared with butter, like a cook's. Dickens used the term in The Pickwick Papers in 1836.
chauffeur		The term chauffeur comes from the French term for stoker because the earliest automobiles, like their railroad and sea vessel counterparts, were steam-powered and required the driver to stoke the engine.
disaster		The root of the word disaster ("bad star" in Greek) comes from an astrological sense of a calamity blamed on the position of planets.
Don't throw out the baby with the bathwater.		This saying comes from a German proverb. The earliest printed reference is in Thomas Murner's satirical work Narrenbeschwörung (Appeal to Fools), dated 1512.

quarantine		Ships arriving in Venice from infected ports were required to sit at anchor for 40 days before landing. This practice, called quarantine, was derived from the Italian words quaranta giorni, which mean "40 days."
quiz		The story goes that a Dublin theater proprietor by the name of Richard Daly made a bet that he could, within 48 hours, make a nonsense word known throughout the city and that the public would supply a meaning for it.
whiskey/whisky— why are there two spellings?		The Scots spell it whisky, and the Irish spell it whiskey with an e. This difference in the spelling comes from the translations of the word from the Scottish and Irish Gaelic forms. Whiskey with the e is also used when referring to American whiskies.

States, Abbreviations, and Flags

ABBREVIATION	STATE	DRAW THE FLAG	FAMOUS SONG	SINGER/GROUP
AR	Arkansas		"Mary Queen of Arkansas"	Bruce Springsteen
IN	Indiana		"Small Town"	John Mellencamp
KS	Kansas		"Wichita Lineman"	Glen Campbell
LA	Louisiana		"House of the Rising Sun"	The Animals
MN	Minnesota		"Say Shh"	Atmosphere
NE	Nebraska		"Omaha"	Counting Crows

NJ	New Jersey		"Jersey Girl"	Bruce Springsteen
NM	New Mexico		"Albuquerque"	Neil Young
NV	Nevada		"Waking Up in Vegas"	Katy Perry
SC	South Carolina		"Hickory Wind"	The Byrds
UT	Utah		"Salt Lake City"	The Beach Boys
WV	West Virginia		"Take Me Home Country Roads"	John Denver

Resources

Websites: United States and Canada

American Dyslexia Association Blog

    dyslexia.me

Dyslexic Advantage

    dyslexicadvantage.org

Dyslexia Canada

    dyslexiacanada.org/resources

Dyslexia Software

    ghotit.com

Helping Adults with Dyslexia

    readinghorizons.com/dyslexia/dyslexia-interventions/helping-adults-with-dyslexia

How Dyslexia Is Diagnosed After High School

    understood.org/en/learning-thinking-differences/child-learning-disabilities /dyslexia/how-dyslexia-is-diagnosed-after-high-school

International Dyslexia Association

    dyslexiaida.org

International Dyslexia Association Ontario: Formal Assessment of Dyslexia

    idaontario.com/assessment-for-dyslexia

Job Accommodation Network

    askjan.org

Learning Disabilities Association of America

    ldaamerica.org/adults

Nessy State-Specific Dyslexia Laws

    nessy.com/us/state-dyslexia-legislation

Text to Speech Reader (You have to listen to a reader reading the book, but it is a good idea if you also follow it in print while listening.)

    ttsreader.com

Three Dyslexia Programs for Adults

    readandspell.com/dyslexia-programs-for-adults

Tips for Increasing Reading Speed

    ghc.edu/sites/default/files/StudentResources/documents/learningcenter
    /handouts/Reading/increase_reading_speed.pdf

Unlocking the Reading Code

    unlockingthereadingcode.com

Visual Images of Dyslexia

    pinterest.ca/drawspoodles/resources-for-dyslexic-adults

What Musicians Can Tell Us About Dyslexia and the Brain

    dyslexiaonline.com/blog/musicians-can-tell-us-dyslexia-brain

The Yale Center for Dyslexia and Creativity

    dyslexia.yale.edu

Articles, Books, and Audiobooks

Castillo, Anabel, and Jeffrey W. Gilger. "Adult Perceptions of Children with Dyslexia in the USA." *Annals of Dyslexia* 68 (2018): 203–17. link.springer.com/article/10.1007/s11881-018-0163-0.

Chase, Cheryl. "Dyslexia and Resilience in Adults: A Psychologist's Perspective." *Dyslexia Connection* 9, no. 2 (2019). dyslexiaida.org/dyslexia-and-resilience-in-adults-a-psychologists-perspective.

Eide, Brock L., and Fernette F. Eide. *Dyslexic Advantage: Unlocking the Hidden Potential of the Dyslexic Brain.* New York: Hudson Street Press, 2011. (available as an audiobook)

Hicks, John. "Let's Talk about Adult Dyslexia." October 11, 2019. youtube.com/watch?v=iE0tWaMoC6o.

Other Countries

Australia

Australian Dyslexia Association

    dyslexiaassociation.org.au/adults

Dyslexia Correction Program

    focusonlearning.com.au/adult-dyslexia.html

Learning Difference Convention

    learningdifferenceconvention.com

New Zealand

Services for Adults

    speld.org.nz/services-for-adults

Understanding Dyslexia

    dyslexiafoundation.org.nz/d_assessment.html

Understanding the World of Adult Dyslexics

    educationcentral.co.nz/understanding-the-world-of-adult-dyslexics

United Kingdom

Adult Dyslexia Organisation

    checkthemap.org

British Dyslexia Association

    bdadyslexia.org.uk/advice/adults

Dysguise

    dysguise.com/free-resources

Dyslexia Action

    dyslexiaaction.org.uk

The Dyslexia Association

    dyslexia.uk.net/adults-with-dyslexia

Dyslexia Help

    dyslexiahelp.co.uk/search.aspx

Dyslexia Scotland

dyslexiascotland.org.uk/our-adult-networks

Grooops Dyslexia Aware Counseling

grooops.org

Helen Arkell Dyslexia Charity

helenarkell.org.uk

References

Eide, Fernette. "Dyslexia Laws 2020." *Dyslexic Advantage*. Accessed August 3, 2020. dyslexicadvantage.org/dyslexia-laws-2018.

Frith, Uta. "Resolving the Paradoxes of Dyslexia." in *Dyslexia and Literacy*, edited by G. Reid and J. Wearmouth, 45–68. Chichester, UK: John Wiley and Sons, 2002.

Hoke, John. "Paving the Way to the Future: Opening General Session." Reading, Literacy and Learning Conference, International Dyslexia Association, Portland OR, November 7, 2019.

Kershner, John R. "The Need for a Valid Theory of Dyslexia." *Brain Disorders and Therapy* 4, no. 179 (2015). doi:10.4172/2168-975X.1000179.

"Let's Paint Pompey." Accessed August 3, 2020. letspaintpompey.com/the-journey-begins.

National Reading Panel. "Teaching Children to Read: An Evidence-Based Assessment of the Scientific Research Literature on Reading and Its Implications for Reading Instruction." February 27, 2000. nichd.nih.gov/sites/default/files/publications/pubs/nrp/Documents/report.pdf.

Nessy. "Dyslexia Legislation by State." Last modified January 16, 2019. nessy.com/us/state -dyslexia-legislation.

Nicolson, Roderick I., and Angela J. Fawcett. "Positive Dyslexia: Towards a Dyslexia Friendly Society." In *The Dyslexia Handbook*. Bracknell, UK: BDA, 2020.

Reid, Gavin. *Dyslexia: A Practitioners Handbook*. 5th ed. Chichester, UK: John Wiley and Sons, 2016.

Ridyard, Aidan. "Reflecting on a Life with Dyslexia." In *The Dyslexia Handbook*. Bracknell, UK: BDA, 2019.

Sawchuk, Stephen. "Influential Reading Group Makes It Clear: Students Need Systematic, Explicit Phonics." *Education Week Teaching Now* (blog). July 18, 2019. blogs.edweek .org/teachers/teaching_now/2019/07/influential_reading_group_makes_it_clear_students _need_systematic_explicit_phonics.html.

Shaywitz, Sally. *Overcoming Dyslexia: A New and Complete Science-Based Program for Reading Problems at Any Level*. Rev. ed. New York: Alfred Knopf, 2009.

Stewart, Jackie. *Winning Is Not Enough*. London: Headline Publishing Group, 2009.

West, Thomas G. *In the Mind's Eye: Visual Thinkers, Gifted People with Dyslexia and Other Learning Difficulties, Computer Images, and the Ironies of Creativity*. New York: Prometheus Books, 1997.

West, Thomas G. *Thinking Like Einstein*, New York: Prometheus Books, 2004.

Wolf, Maryanne, Alyssa G. O'Rourke, Calvin Gidney, Maureen Lovett, Paul Cirino, and Robin Morris. "The Second Deficit: An Investigation of the Independence of Phonological and Naming-Speed Deficits in Developmental Dyslexia." *Reading and Writing* 15 (2002): 43–72.

Index

Acknowledgments

I wish to thank Jenn Clark for discussion and advice on chapter 2 and for her support throughout the writing of this book. Thanks also to photographer Rodger Shearer for submitting photographs for an activity. I am of course hugely indebted to my close friends and colleagues past and present who have supported and encouraged me throughout my career.

About the Author

 **Gavin Reid, PhD,** is an international psychologist and author. He was a high school teacher for 10 years and university lecturer for 15 years and has written more than 30 books in the field of dyslexia and learning. His books have been translated into seven languages, and some are in third, fourth, and fifth editions. He lectures worldwide and provides regular international consultancies. Dr. Reid is chair of the British Dyslexia Association Accreditation Board and a regular speaker at the International Dyslexia Association in the United States. He is a director of the Literacy Intervention and Training Group (the LIT Group) in West Vancouver, Canada. He has been involved in a number of research programs and consultancies focusing on adults with dyslexia and has sat on government panels on assessment and dyslexia. He has also been engaged in UN-funded projects as a learning differences expert and has appeared on a number of radio and television programs on dyslexia worldwide. Dr. Reid is passionate about helping to achieve equal opportunities for those with dyslexia and is a strong advocate of the strengths and positive aspects of dyslexia. He resides in Vancouver, Canada.